Stories to Grow On

STORIES TO GROW ON

*Demonstrations of Language
Learning in K–8 Classrooms*

edited by
JULIE M. JENSEN

HEINEMANN
PORTSMOUTH, N.H.

Heinemann Educational Books, Inc.
70 Court Street   Portsmouth, NH   03801
Offices and agents throughout the world

© 1989 by Heinemann Educational Books, Inc. All rights reserved. No part of this book may be reproduced in any form or by electronic or mechanical means, including information storage and retrieval systems, without permission in writing from the publisher, except by a reviewer, who may quote brief passages in a review.

The publishers and authors wish to thank the children, teachers, and parents whose words and writings are quoted here for permission to reproduce them, and to the following for permission to quote from previously published works:
Thomas C. Cooper, *Horticulture* 63 (March 1985), page 2. Reprinted by permission of *Horticulture* magazine.
Umberto Eco, "How I Wrote *The Name of the Rose*," *The New York Times Book Review*, October 10, 1984. Copyright © 1984 by The New York Times Company. Reprinted by permission.
John Barth, "Writing: Can It Be Taught?", *The New York Times Book Review*, June 16, 1985. Copyright © 1985 by The New York Times Company. Reprinted by permission.
Lloyd Alexander, "High Fantasy and Heroic Romance," *The Horn Book* 47 (1971). Reprinted by permission of the author.
Every effort has been made to contact the copyright holders and the children and their parents for permission to reprint borrowed material. We regret any oversights that may have occurred and would be happy to rectify them in future printings of this work.

LIBRARY OF CONGRESS
Library of Congress Cataloging-in-Publication Data

Stories to grow on: demonstrations of language learning in K–8
    classrooms / edited by Julie M. Jensen.
        p. cm.
    Includes bibliographies.
    ISBN 0-435-08482-8
    1. Language arts (Elementary)—United States—Congresses.
2. English language—Study and teaching (Elementary)—United States—
Congresses.   I. Jensen, Julie M.
LB1576.S7995   1989
372.6—dc 19   88–17601
                                                                         CIP

Cover by Max-Karl Winkler.
Printed in the United States of America.

10 9 8 7 6 5 4 3 2 1

Dedicated to our colleagues and friends who represented secondary schools and colleges at the Conference of the Coalition of English Associations— in the spirit of all-level cooperation and understanding.

Contents

PROLOGUE	John C. Maxwell	ix
INTRODUCTION	Julie M. Jensen	xv
PART I	**The Conference Report**	
1	Language Arts for the 21st Century: A Vision for Elementary School English Teaching from the Coalition of English Associations Conference *William H. Teale*	3
PART II	**Teachers Telling Their Stories**	
2	From the First: Teaching to Diversity *Carol S. Avery*	37
3	Kids and Computers: Who's on First? *C. Jane Hydrick*	57
4	Thinking Throughout the Process: Self-Evaluation in Writing *Susan Stires*	71
5	Writing What They Read: Reflections on Literature and Child Writers *Fredrick R. Burton*	97
6	Excuse Me, Where's Your Teacher? *Donna Carrara*	117
7	Constructing a Mosaic in the Context of Cultural Diversity *Mary M. Kitagawa*	131
8	Encouraging Sixth-Grade Historians *Diane T. Orchard*	147
9	Reading, Writing, Rappin', and Rollin' Your Own *Mary Mercer Krogness*	157
EPILOGUE: Memories to Grow On	*Julie M. Jensen*	169
THE AUTHORS		179

Prologue
JOHN C. MAXWELL

The stories in this volume were stimulated in part by an invitational conference held in Maryland in the summer of 1987. The conference was the culmination of four years of cooperation and planning, particularly among leaders of the National Council of Teachers of English and the Modern Language Association. NCTE, with 55,000 individual members, and MLA, with 27,000, are major subject-matter associations that seek to influence scholarship and instruction in the English language arts through publications, conferences, and other means. While the membership of MLA consists solely of college and university professors of English and other modern languages, NCTE membership is composed of teachers and specialists from elementary grades through graduate school.

From time to time in recent decades, NCTE and MLA have come together in cooperative efforts to review the curriculum and content of instruction in English and the language arts. Each time, the hope has been that by intensive study of the field, we might achieve new insights and provide new directions for teachers and others concerned about this most central subject matter in schools and colleges.

Prologue

The first major instance of such cooperation occurred in the late 1950s when, in what is now recognized as the Sputnik era, American scholars and teachers became concerned about what some believed was a "falling away from standards" and a denial of the centrality of solid subject matter in the education of children and youth. Such writers as Rudolph Flesch, Arthur Bestor, and Bernard Iddings Bell had written scathing criticisms of the schools earlier in the decade under such titles as *Crisis in Education* (Bell 1949), *Educational Wastelands* (Bestor 1953), and *Why Johnny Can't Read* (Flesch 1955). By and large, these works took issue with what the authors believed were hostile influences on education: permissiveness, flabby scholarship among teachers, and "life adjustment education," which was falsely ascribed to John Dewey and his disciples.

While most educators were sure that the accounts in these books and the many contemporary articles in the same vein were inaccurate and possibly hysterical, there was enough clamor to inspire the leaders of NCTE and MLA to seek funds to bring teachers and scholars together in a series of meetings in 1958 to identify and discuss a set of some thirty issues in the teaching of English. The so-called Basic Issues Conferences, which stretched over a series of weekend meetings, involved NCTE, MLA, the College English Association, and the American Studies Association. The final report (*The Basic Issues in the Teaching of English*, 1958), which was widely distributed among schools and colleges, took an affirmative stance on academic concerns but was marked more by its discussion of unresolved questions in the profession than by any resolution of issues concerning what should be taught and when and how.

The *Basic Issues* report, and the connections among scholars and teachers it helped to strengthen, also served to set the stage for an academically oriented effort in the early 1960s that culminated in Project English curriculum development activities at a number of colleges and universities, and in several years of English Institutes designed to enhance the subject-matter preparation of experienced elementary and secondary teachers of English and the language arts.

"New English," as the revised outlook was sometimes called, suggested that another milestone conference was needed, both to examine the trends of the preceding decade and to determine whether new directions were called for. Again, the NCTE and the MLA were the principal organizers, this time of a conference held at Dartmouth College in the summer of 1966. Because the work of scholars and teachers in Great Britain and Canada was thought to have potential significance to American schools, educational leaders from those two countries were also invited to the conference. The four-week meeting of some forty-eight persons, financed by a grant from the Carnegie Corporation, was marked by a collision between the subject-centered advocates of the New English and the child-centered enthusiasts from Great Britain.

Two books emerged from the conference, the most notable and the most influential being *Growth through English* (1967) by John Dixon of England. Through the years, the Dixon book has influenced thousands of teachers and teacher educators. Coincidental with its publication came the Great Society proclaimed by President Johnson, the rallying cry for efforts to help the socially and educationally "disadvantaged" in our society. The effect of Dixon's book was to reinforce the growing trend to make education personally meaningful and enriching to individuals who were apathetic about schooling. The term "relevance" became a touchstone for efforts to find and use literature that would speak powerfully and intimately to young people. Although it was later alleged by critics of this period that teachers forgot about standards, that "anything went," and that subject-matter learning was an insufficient objective of instruction in English, many teachers worked hard to make their classrooms as responsive to student interests as they could.

Whatever the cause, the curriculum did open up. In secondary schools, the range of literature used in English classes broadened substantially. Courses like English III (which usually had no definition) gave way to theme-centered semester courses on, for example, film study, the literature of minority groups, or the study of death through literature. This "elective" movement was not universally followed in schools, but it had a substantial influence on curriculum materials used everywhere. Inevitably, there would be a backlash, and it came in the form of "accountability" and "basic skills" instructional objectives urged and even demanded by school boards and state legislatures. The people, it was said, wanted a greater return on their educational dollar, and as the economic base for schools tightened during the 1970s, further claims were made that education, and particularly education in the English language arts, had failed to produce the literate citizenry needed for a modern democracy. Worse yet, it was claimed that educational achievement in this country had fallen to such a low level that we were threatened in the marketplace by European and Third World competitors.

In the early 1980s, various prestigious groups, as well as the federal government, initiated studies of our educational system to determine what was wrong and what needed to be done. The first of these, *A Nation at Risk* (1983), proclaimed a crisis in American education and proposed that schools and teachers needed to provide more "rigor" in the education of children and youth. Like subsequent reports it called for "standards," "subject-matter competence," more homework, the end of "social promotion" and a variety of other reforms designed to "toughen" the schools.

Prologue

This, in brief, was the context that prompted a new effort by NCTE and MLA to call, once again, for a summit conference of leaders in the field to assess the state of English language arts teaching and attempt to provide direction for the profession in the 1990s and beyond. Leaders of NCTE and MLA had been meeting informally and occasionally in the late 1970s and early 1980s, more or less to keep in touch. Sometime in 1984, the idea for a new "Dartmouth" conference to examine the English language arts curriculum and its teaching emerged. Phyllis Franklin of the MLA prepared a proposal for a meeting to set plans for a conference to study English and its teaching, which was submitted to the Rockefeller and Exxon Education Foundations. The leaders of a new group, the Coalition of English Associations, met in August 1984 to determine the broad objectives of such a conference and discuss how it might proceed for the benefit of the profession.

By this time the Coalition consisted of not only NCTE and MLA but also the Association of Departments of English, the College English Association, and the College Language Association, as well as an NCTE constituent organization, the Conference on College Composition and Communication. Subsequently, the Coalition would involve two more NCTE constituent groups: the Conference on English Education (teacher educators, for the most part) and the Conference of Secondary School English Department Chairs.

Through the efforts of Phyllis Franklin, initial funding for the conference was promised by late 1986, and plans were set for a three-week meeting in the summer of 1987 at the Aspen Institute for Humanistic Studies on Maryland's Eastern Shore. Ultimately, the foundations and agencies that supported the conference included the Andrew W. Mellon Foundation and the National Endowment for the Humanities as well as the Rockefeller Foundation and the Exxon Education Foundation.

What was remarkable and different about the 1987 meeting was first, the substantial cadre of elementary teachers and language arts specialists who attended, in contrast with the almost total absence of such professionals at the 1958 and 1966 conferences. Second was the presence of a large cadre of practicing teachers in the elementary and secondary schools. Nearly a third of the participants in 1987 were "from the firing line," as some of them were inclined to say. In the previous conferences—and in the bodies preparing the reform reports of the 1980s in general—classroom teachers had almost never participated in appreciable numbers.

The second notable phenomenon at the 1987 meeting was the profound influence exerted on the secondary school and college groups by the cadre of elementary school teachers and college specialists in the language arts. This Elementary Section, to call it that, was a body of fifteen individuals who met each day and quickly developed a clear vision of the kind of schooling needed for children today and tomorrow. For part of each day at the conference, these fifteen also worked with groups of secondary and college teachers and thus had a major effect on the flow of thinking about education at those levels. High school and college teachers were greatly interested in the views of the elementary teachers and specialists. By the midpoint of the conference, a number of the collegians articulated their own, perhaps subordinated, perception that students learn best when they are involved in shaping the goals, the contexts, and the methods of their own instruction. Considerable time was spent in secondary and college groups pondering the appropriateness of learner-centered, integrated, and interactive models of instruction at all levels of education.

The final chapters in the story of the Coalition Conference are yet to come. This book is but one chapter. Two others are also being written, and they will embody their authors' perceptions of the 1987 conference and conclusions about teaching and learning in the language arts. Those who have written this part of the story were among the prime movers at the conference, and their thoughts will also be manifest in the other books. To a degree, the story of the English Coalition Conference is the story of the teachers and specialists whose words and ideas appear in the pages that follow.

REFERENCES

The Basic Issues in the Teaching of English. 1958. Urbana, Ill.: National Council of Teachers of English.

Bell, Bernard Iddings. 1949. *Crisis in Education.* New York: McGraw-Hill.

Bestor, Arthur. 1953. *Educational Wastelands.* Urbana, Ill.: University of Illinois Press.

Dixon, John, ed. 1967. *Growth through English.* Reading, England: National Association for the Teaching of English.

Flesch, Rudolph. 1955. *Why Johnny Can't Read.* New York: Harper.

National Commission on Excellence in Education. 1983. *A Nation at Risk.* Washington, D.C.: U.S. Department of Education.

Introduction
JULIE M. JENSEN

The value of stories for enriching the lives of children is limitless. But just as children can be transformed through the power of story, so too can teachers. Stories are a source of pleasure and insight, capable of lifting teachers, like anyone else, from their individual experiences into the world of the storyteller. Through stories, teachers can gain new perspectives on their own environments and the people who inhabit them. They can see how others live and how they respond to important questions in their lives; they can recognize themselves in stories—their beliefs and attitudes, hopes and fears. Stories can launch a quest for self-discovery. The reader of a tale, faced with its puzzlements and problems, comes to ask, Where do I stand? What would I do? How could I do better? *Stories to Grow On* invites teachers to make connections with the lives of its authors and to join them in a long, continuing story of professional growth.

We have tried to create elaborated instances of "goodness" in teaching, each one intended to be a stepping-stone for growth. Our stories stand in stark contrast to the familiar fact-and-figure laden rhetoric intended to establish pathology in education. The power of the stories teachers can tell lies in their richness of detail. Stories provide nuance, they embed ideas and practices in familiar contexts, they account for the importance of affect, they clarify relationships, they communicate in everyday language to diverse audiences, they persuade people to think about complicated issues, they are holistic and comprehensive statements, they are hopeful, empathetic, and confidence-building. By viewing teachers as primary informants, as reflective and wise practitioners, by identifying teachers with vision and using their stories as a vehicle for knowing and changing, we can compose a picture of good teaching. Where else but in teachers' tales will we find the specifics of school life, specifics that will allow the identification of general patterns?

Stories are, at long last, coming into their own as a text—a data base—for researchers. While it has not been fashionable to value the "wisdom of practice" as a source of knowledge about teaching, even those researchers who do not consider the elementary classroom their home are beginning to ask good teachers what they believe, understand, and know how to do that enables them to teach well. Best of all, the line between teacher and researcher is growing less visible. The documented observations and conclusions of those who have daily contact with children in classrooms are making substantial contributions to the professional literature. The result may be that detailed portrayals of expertise in teaching will be less rare. Lee Shulman is one who has been conducting "wisdom of practice" studies. The descriptions of excellent teaching he has been gathering will become the basis for principles of good practice, which in turn will yield guidelines for educational improvement. Pointing out the extensive but unarticulated knowledge of practitioners, Shulman wrote in the February 1987 *Harvard Educational Review*, "A major portion of the research agenda for the next decade will be to collect, collate, and interpret the practical knowledge of teachers for the purpose of establishing a case literature and codifying its principles, precedents, and parables."

The story of the Conference of the Coalition of English Associations is a graphic example of both the practical and theoretical wisdom of elementary classroom teachers. Their presence was critical to the success of the conference. Among their contributions was an ability to support their views with concrete examples of sound practices and school realities. Time and time again they helped others understand why and how to put students first—before a textbook, a test, a favored literary work, a trusted teaching method. They patiently and persistently demonstrated how knowledge about children's language and learning forms the foundation for decisions about goals, curriculum, and methods. For them, it was not good enough to talk about schooling in the abstract; they illustrated their

Introduction

stance with specific pictures and stories of effective language arts classrooms. Near the close of the conference seven prominent English educators were asked, "What influence do you think elementary teachers have had on this conference?" Their responses are an indication of the spirit of this book:

> *[You influenced us] by both talking about and exemplifying the special combination of emotional and cognitive engagement that we have all ended up trying to express.*
> —Wayne Booth

> *A profound one! The emphasis on "teaching children," "student-centered learning," "the construction of meaning," etc.... helped to move me beyond my normal ways of thinking.*
> —Robert Denham

> *A strong injection of child-centered approaches.*
> —Peter Elbow

> *A humanizing effect. Elementary teachers have always focused upon the learner as inquirer; they are unifiers and synthesizers.*
> —Janet Emig

> *They changed the views of many, especially college people, about what it means to teach a child. They provided access to the notions about learning and individually designed programs of learning. They established the emphasis on interaction.*
> —Richard Lloyd-Jones

> *The strong elementary presence here has confirmed the intellectually rigorous demands made on elementary teachers and it has led the way in allowing us not only to talk about but to* experience *literature.*
> —Andrea Lunsford

> *A profound influence. The concepts of language arts, interactive learning, and student-centered teaching have dominated the conference.*
> —Robert Scholes

Introduction

Because this book is not only a collection of stories about the good works of individual teachers but also the story of how these teachers worked together at a significant conference, a word about process is in order. Phyllis Franklin, Executive Director of the Modern Language Association, reflected on the conference in the Fall 1987 *MLA Newsletter*. She emphasized that schools should provide a special place—and a critical opportunity—for children to learn; that the ideal classroom is a rich and supportive environment for learners actively engaged in reading, writing, speaking, and listening; that the teacher's task is to create situations and provide materials that encourage inquiry, practice in the use of language, and interaction; and that teachers must also serve as model learners and users of language. As the person most responsible for the success of the conference, Phyllis Franklin is evidence that the best in an English language arts teacher is also the best in a conference coordinator. We had that special place to learn—The Aspen Institute for Humanistic Studies located on the Eastern Shore of Maryland. We had a critical opportunity for learning—three uninterrupted weeks in July 1987 "to develop a new national consensus on the teaching of English in American schools and colleges and to make recommendations about future directions for instruction at all levels of education." Our environment was rich in natural beauty, and we had the constant support of sixty bright, committed, and congenial learners. We were so actively involved in listening, speaking, reading, and writing that local duplicating machines could not bear the strain. And situations were created that encouraged our inquiry and constant interaction. For an unrivaled learning experience we thank Phyllis, a committee of representatives from the eight English Associations composing the Coalition, the National Endowment for the Humanities, and the Exxon, Mellon, and Rockefeller Foundations.

Stories to Grow On enlarges the work of the fifteen conferees representing language arts teaching at the elementary school level, most of them elementary classroom teachers. It is a way to sustain a point of view on which we were united—that kindergarten through grade eight classrooms can have environments that are in harmony with what we understand about how children learn language. Our book has two parts. In Part 1, William Teale presents the final conference report of the elementary group, which was composed of the eleven authors represented here, plus Rosalinda Barrera, Rudine Sims Bishop, Vera Milz, and Faith Schullstrom. In a lengthy postscript, Teale looks back to a milestone conference held during the 1960s, both for perspective and for direction. Part 2 tells a series of eight stories that collectively illuminate our shared conference experience. In the margins of these chapters, major points from the conference report are highlighted as they are illustrated in the stories.

In the opening story, Carol Avery tells about the first day of school in her first-grade classroom. From that day forward, children listen to and talk about books, and they read and write in book-filled surroundings. "The books represent a curriculum with children's literature at its foundation and the needs of children at its heart."

C. Jane Hydrick describes how her second graders use computers in their study of Native Americans. Because computers help them to manage information, the children are better able to control the content and purpose of their learning. This story profiles lively, independent, challenged, curious, and confident learners.

Susan Stires tells a story about primary-grade learning disabled students who demonstrate their ability to write and to evaluate their writing. Like the other teachers in this book, Stires is an active learner along with her students.

Fred Burton's third- and fourth-grade classroom is the setting for his observations of how children borrow from and improvise on their literary experiences when they write.

The collaborative relationship Donna Carrara establishes with her fourth graders continues as the students move through the grades. She is a supportive partner in learning who describes the sources of her support.

Mary Kitagawa's story is set in her half Mexican American, half Native American sixth-grade classroom. Through varied and personally interesting experiences, students talk, read, and write their way to a better understanding of their own and other cultures.

Diane Orchard tells how her sixth-grade students listen, speak, read, and write in order to learn and share information about their state's history. Using primary sources, the students raise questions and find answers. Their learning is interdisciplinary, personal, involving, and enjoyable.

Mary Krogness is a teacher with a challenge, and a philosophical commitment to match. Her story about a middle school classroom is stirring, upsetting, suspenseful, hopeful, and humane. It reveals a quest for student engagement and an ability to look for small victories. Talk is central in this classroom: "Talk is, after all, the heart of the matter; it is also a matter of the heart."

In a brief prologue, John Maxwell, Executive Director of the National Council of Teachers of English, conference organizer, and member of the elementary group, places the conference in a historical context dating to the late 1950s. In doing so he tells a story of interorganizational coop-

Introduction

eration on behalf of English language arts teaching and learning. Finally, in an epilogue, I suggest that stories to grow on can be rooted not only in our experiences as teachers but in recollections of our own best teachers.

Our work at the Conference exemplified a humane, learner-centered, inquiring, risk-taking, and highly interactive process. Yet our product, comprising Part I of this book, will be recognized by good teachers as sensible, obvious, and familiar. Little that we thought or said or wrote is remarkable for its novelty. What is remarkable is the scant attention to principles we stand by in vast numbers of today's elementary school classrooms. For that reason, we do not depend on a report to have power over practice. This is a book about the power of story, and its centerpiece is eight stories by teachers, for teachers. In these *Stories to Grow On* are our hopes for language learners.

Stories to Grow On

THE CONFERENCE REPORT

part I

> ...*the great thing in this world is not so much where we stand, as in what direction we are moving: To reach the port...we must sail sometimes with the wind and sometimes against it—but we must sail, and not drift, nor lie at anchor.*
> —Oliver Wendell Holmes
>   The Autocrat of the Breakfast Table

1

Language Arts for the 21st Century

A Vision for Elementary School English Teaching from the Coalition of English Associations Conference

WILLIAM H. TEALE

The broad goal of the Coalition of English Associations Conference was to suggest directions for English studies in the United States and thereby promote discussion of the teaching of English among members of the education profession and the community at large. The elementary representatives among the conferees numbered fifteen and included eight elementary school classroom teachers, four university teacher educators, two school district administrative personnel, and one staff member of the National Council of Teachers of English. Over the three weeks of the conference this group worked to construct its vision of what English teaching in the elementary school should be during the latter part of the twentieth and beginning of the twenty-first centuries.

4 The Conference Report

The group produced a document entitled "Language Arts for the 21st Century: The Crossroads of Possibility and Practice." It contained discussion of four major topics: (1) the nature of the child being taught in today's elementary school, (2) the person we would like to emerge from the elementary school language arts classroom, (3) the language arts curriculum, and (4) the day-to-day organization and running of the language arts classroom. The document concluded with two sets of priorities that require attention if the principles of learning and the practices of language arts teaching embodied in the report are to become widespread in the nation's schools. The first set listed implications for school administrators, teacher educators, and policymakers. The second set proposed research priorities. The entire document was adopted in principle by conferees at the close of the conference.

In this chapter, I present the elementary strand's conclusions about effective language arts instruction in the schools of America although I do not reproduce the actual report fashioned at the conference; it was intended only as a working document and was written in a short time. In the present account, however, I have attempted to convey the content and the spirit of the recommendations put forth by the group, and I have preserved the language of the original to the extent possible.

I have also taken the liberty of providing commentary from two perspectives on the report itself. On the one hand, I try to describe some of the processes that led to the conclusions of the elementary group members and of the conference overall. I feel that this reflection on how the report evolved will help the reader better understand the significance of these recommendations for the profession. Also, in the final section of the chapter I take a retrospective look at the last major consideration of the status of the teaching of English, the Dartmouth Conference of 1966. Such a historical perspective can help us see how things have and have not changed in the past twenty years. It also suggests what effect the present report may have on the teaching of children. Overall, then, my aim is to help the reader understand the what and why of the English Coalition perspective on language arts education in the elementary schools of the United States.

Language Arts for the 21st Century

The task set for conferees at the Coalition meeting was to consider four general topics: (1) changes in students and curriculum during the past two decades, (2) goals for the teaching of English, (3) the teaching and learning of various aspects of English (language, writing, reading literature and other texts), and (4) teacher education. We talked over these topics, as members of both the elementary strand discussion group and groups composed of representatives of all three levels of schooling—elementary, secondary, and college. In a relatively short time it became apparent that a remarkable singularity in perspective existed among the individuals in the elementary strand. Though there were differences on particulars and differences of style among the fifteen individuals, we thought alike on the major issues of curriculum, instruction, materials, and assessment in language arts. Perhaps more important for the conference overall, each of us in his or her own way harped on the centrality of the child in any discussion of what English studies should be or how English should be taught.

Why this similarity in perspective existed I do not know. The members came from various parts of the United States and had learned their professions in different settings with a variety of intellectual traditions. But we did share certain commonalities. Several members knew each other or had worked together before the conference. A still larger number had "met" each other through professional publications. Many of the members had worked in some capacity with Writing Projects. All of us, in some way or other, were deeply involved in promoting the use of literature in teaching children to read, write, speak, and listen. But whatever the actual reasons, it remains that the report represents a strong consensus among the conferees about the nature of English teaching in the American elementary school.

Each topic the elementary strand addressed is presented in this chapter in the order in which it appeared in the report.

Today's Elementary School Child

Two factors especially shaped the discussion about students in elementary school today and in coming decades. One was the demographic facts about our constituency. In short, the population of elementary school children will become increasingly diverse over the next two decades. The trend toward an increase in the proportion of children from single-parent homes, in evidence over the past decade and a half, will continue in the coming years. The percentage of children from ethnic minorities will continue to increase through the year 2000, and projections indicate that the population consisting of individuals from ethnic "minorities" will become the majority in all of the major metropolitan areas across the United States. The changing nature of the school population has important implications for any recommendations on the teaching of English in the elementary school.

The other factor was a concerted effort by many in attendance to guard against a false nostalgia. It seems that in a variety of ways every generation looks back to prior eras with a "they don't make 'em like that any more" attitude. Certainly this attitude has affected the debate about education in the United States. It is not difficult to find columnists, book writers, and politicians conjuring up the good old days to make a point. In the latter half of the 1980s the spate of education reform movements has brought with it a sense that we used to do it right but don't anymore. The reaction against this point of view was nowhere more evident than in discussion with and about E. D. Hirsch, Jr. and his notion of cultural literacy (Hirsch 1987). Though Hirsch himself does not play upon nostalgia, the cultural literacy "movement" carries with it a "let's get back to" attitude. As the members of the elementary strand discussed the nature of the elementary school child, we expressed great concern that the influences of the past twenty years be considered both for their positive effect on the children who attend our schools and for their negative impact on children's participation in education. Thus, we consciously strove to present a realistic view of the student population, not one overwhelmed by the great changes of the past two decades that mourned the passing of the good old days.

We concluded that America's elementary school population today resembles a rich, vibrant mosaic—a dynamic composite of children from a variety of cultures, linguistic backgrounds, and religions. Children's ways of knowing and learning reflect changes in society, in family, and in technology. Some of these changes have influenced children and their learning in positive ways, while other changes have been detrimental.

Many of the *changes in society* pose challenges for today's schools and the children they serve. For example, frequent and extensive geographical redistribution of children and their families, both across the country and from rural to urban areas, has resulted in constantly changing school populations. Variations in student population have brought together students of many races, languages, and religious persuasions, which, on the one hand, has been enriching, exposing students to many different perspectives. On the other hand, the same changes have also been frustrating for those children who have been uprooted from familiar surroundings and who may therefore experience a sense of isolation.

Changes in family structure and lifestyle affect children from all economic backgrounds. In many family settings now prevalent, it is difficult to meet the needs of children. Families with limited financial resources, who have greater difficulty providing for basic needs such as food, clothing, and shelter, now comprise a larger proportion of the national population. Larger numbers of children are coming to school hungry, malnourished, or tired. In increasing numbers of families, the quality and frequency of personal interaction and communication have been reduced. In some instances, there are not enough adults to go around; in others, family members are overscheduled in their activities and have little time left for interacting with one another. Frequently also, contemporary lifestyles emphasize materialistic values and self-gratification, thereby detracting from both the time for and the quality of interaction between children and their families. Therefore, children today often carry heavy emotional burdens that drain their intellectual and creative energy. They may receive little encouragement and few opportunities for imagining and creating.

Changes in technology have also significantly affected today's students. Children are increasingly immersed in media and technology, a state of affairs that is a mixed blessing. Media expose children to a large stock of information and images, and technological innovations provide many avenues for manipulating that information. Media may also encourage reading by presenting literary selections in inviting formats, but unmonitored listening and viewing may involve large chunks of time and yield undesirable results. Children are therefore often sophisticated in their awareness of the world around them and in their ability to use modern technology, but their increasing use of media may leave them less time for active participation in other ways of knowing. It may also change the ways children handle problems; for instance, they may see violence as a solution and look for the "quick fixes" so often enacted in thirty-minute program formats.

These changes create some serious problems for children, but the combination of these factors also gives us children with a stronger sense of peer support (they care about one another), an extensive store of information, and a less stereotyped view of the world than that held by their counterparts of fifteen to twenty years ago.

Goals for the Teaching of English in the Elementary School

Consideration of the nature of today's elementary school child led naturally to the next focus of attention, the goals for the teaching of English. In retrospect it is possible to see that this topic proved a turning point for the elementary strand. The subject of goals arose on the third day of the conference, and it was not resolved until the final days of the meeting. The elementary, secondary, and college strands each addressed the topic of goals independently, as did the three cross-level strands. By Thursday of the first week there were goal statements in the minutes or reports of all six strands.

A subcommittee composed of representatives of all levels was formed to bring coherence to the goal statements. This subcommittee synthesized all the statements to create a document that was presented to the overall conference during the second week. Two characteristics of that first set of goals stand out. First, the goals focused on the necessity for active understanding among students by stressing the importance of three aspects of student learning: knowing about, knowing how to, and knowing why. Second, although the goals were divided into four subcategories—(1) reading, (2) writing, (3) speaking and listening, and (4) content—as the preface to the goals stressed, "we do not imply that they should be taught separately. One of the most vociferous points of agreement among participants was the importance of finding as many ways as possible to merge these domains."

The goals reflected findings from the best of past and recent research. The reading section, for example, emphasized the development of students as voluntary readers who use prior knowledge to comprehend text, read texts critically, and monitor their own reading and interpretive processes, as well as more traditional goals in such areas as decoding and drawing inferences. Writing goals reflected a process orientation and stressed the importance of the new technologies, maintaining that "students should know how to work simultaneously with words and visual images as tools for thinking and communicating." The speaking and listening goals contained little that could be considered truly innovative but did reflect a firm commitment to the importance of these areas, both for their own sake and for their contribution to reading and writing development. The content goals directly addressed the issue of what students should know about English studies. These goals challenged conference participants to consider what texts students should read, what body of information they should know to promote an understanding of what they read, and what they should know about the nature and structure of language. The goals document—four single-spaced pages in all—was circulated to all of the conferees for their consideration.

It quickly became apparent that the subcommittee's attempt to synthesize goal statements was not acceptable to members of the elementary strand. For the elementary members the speaking and listening goals didn't work, and the identification of content goals was problematic. In fact, especially troublesome, despite the disclaimer in the preamble, was the separation of goals into subcategories for reading, writing, and speaking and listening.

Several days and many revisions later a document entitled "The Person We Would Like to Emerge from the Elementary School Classroom" emerged from our talking and writing. There is a great deal in this document that is similar to the original goals statement. The emphasis on knowing about, knowing how to, and knowing why is retained. The important role of metacognition in language and literacy learning is reflected in the goal that centers on students as language theorists. The desire to educate students to *be* readers and writers and not merely to be able to read and write is first on the list of specific goals. But understanding how the revised document differs from the original goals statements is critical to understanding the essence of the overall elementary report and the elementary strand's contribution to the Coalition of English Associations Conference.

Above all, the person—the student—is central in the goals document developed by the elementary group. It is not merely that we have stated language and literacy goals in student-centered terms. Rather, we have attempted to demonstrate that the concern of English instruction in the elementary school is to help individual children develop into confident and capable language users. Directly linked with the emphasis on the individual is the elimination of separate subsections for reading, writing, speaking and listening, and content. The ultimate importance of language and literacy lies in the functions they perform and the uses they serve in an individual's life. The following section presents the goals of the elementary strand.

The Person We Would Like to Emerge from the Elementary School Classroom

Our hope is that when children leave the elementary school, they will be on their way to full participation as citizens in our democracy. We hope that as individuals, they will be caring and compassionate, and respectful of the social and cultural diversity of others. We want them also to be competent, knowledgeable, and self-confident. Since they will live the majority of their lives in the twenty-first century, and we cannot know the specific knowledge they will need, we want them to leave our classrooms with their curiosity, their sense of wonder, and their imagination. With those attributes they will maintain an enthusiasm for learning, both in school and in their homes and communities.

Children who have a lifelong love affair with learning emerge from classrooms in which language and language learning have played a central role. Because language is integral to thinking and to people's interactions with each other, we believe children should leave elementary school *knowing about* language, *knowing how* to read, write, speak, and listen, and *knowing why* language and literacy are so central to their lives. In more specific terms, the language knowledge, abilities, and attitudes that we would like to see develop in our students are as follows:

- *They will be readers and writers*, individuals who find pleasure and satisfaction in reading and writing, and who make those activities an important part of their everyday lives. They will voluntarily engage in reading and writing for their intrinsic social and personal value.
- *They will use language to understand themselves and others and make sense of their world.* As a means of reflecting on their lives, they will engage in such activities as telling and hearing stories, reading novels and poetry, and keeping journals.
- *They will use language as a tool to get things done.* They will use oral language and written language in its varieties as a means of helping them take charge of their lives, express their opinions, and function as productive citizens. Reading, writing, speaking, and listening will, for example, serve to help them succeed in the workplace and conduct other everyday activities like shopping and paying bills. They will, among other things, write letters to editors, read newspapers, fill out forms, speak persuasively.
- *They will leave our classrooms as individuals who know how to read, write, speak, and listen effectively.* As competent language users they will:
  - Use prior knowledge to comprehend new oral or written texts.
  - Possess a variety of strategies for dealing with unfamiliar words and meanings in texts.
  - Respond personally to texts.
  - Comprehend the literal messages in texts.
  - Read and listen interpretively.
  - Read and listen critically.
  - Be able to write in a wide variety of forms for a wide variety of purposes and audiences.
  - Be able to read different types of texts, including poems, essays, stories, and expository text.
  - Make connections within texts and among texts.
  - Use other readers' experiences with, responses to, and interpretations of text.
  - Be able to hear literature, appreciating its sounds and cadences.
- *They will recognize when language is being used to manipulate, coerce,*

or control them, and they will be able to use language as an effective response to such attempts.
- *They will become language theorists*, understanding how they and others around them use oral and written language. In writing they will understand how they develop different pieces and what those pieces do. In reading, they will notice and monitor their own reading processes and their purposes for reading. Self-evaluation is a key component of their oral and written language activities. They will achieve a sense of ownership of their language.
- *They will appreciate and respect the language and culture of others.* They will understand enough about the dynamic nature of language, language change, and language variety to communicate with people of linguistic and cultural groups different from their own. They will have had many opportunities, through reading the literature of various cultural groups and through oral interactions with a variety of people, to be able and willing to see the world from the perspectives of others. They will not only have a sense of the richness and distinctiveness of the life of particular cultural groups, but also a sense of common humanity in the universals of human experience.

These goals summarize the essence of what the elementary strand members believed the teaching of English in the elementary school to be all about. The recommendations for curriculum and activities that follow flow directly from this conception of what students should know and be able to do.

The Language Arts Curriculum

If the child who arrives in the classroom is to emerge as the person just described, the school curriculum and classroom activities must be designed to foster that kind of growth. The elementary strand therefore proposed perspectives on curriculum. These perspectives were necessarily brief and global, given the short time frame in which they were developed and the difficulties inherent in attempting to create curriculum at the national level instead of at the local level, where such decisions should be made. Even with these constraints, however, we recommended certain principles strongly.

First and foremost was the importance of basing curriculum development on a sound research knowledge base. The curriculum should be informed by basic research on child growth and development, on the psychology of language and literacy, and on language and literacy acquisition, as well as by work in learning theory and research on the teaching of language and literacy. The theoretical perspectives of Vygotsky (1978, 1986), Piaget (1926, 1983), Bruner (1977, 1983, 1986), and Dewey (1916, 1963) especially were cited as informing the view of curriculum we espoused.

From such a theoretical base evolved the second major principle: the language arts curriculum should be learner-centered. As Hawkins has put it (1979), the curriculum is something to be uncovered rather than covered. The learner is central to the curriculum and is actively engaged in constructing understandings about language, in learning how to read, write, speak, and listen, and in understanding why language and literacy are important to life in this society.

The learner-centered language arts curriculum emphasizes both content and process (or skills) and treats them as interdependent rather than separate. That is to say, the content of language or literary studies is not regarded merely as an end unto itself but is viewed as serving to enhance development in reading, writing, speaking, and listening. In this way the curriculum is not fragmented into particular pieces of knowledge that are presented to students simply to memorize and subsequently recite or into hundreds of individual skills that are taught and drilled in isolation. A curriculum area like language arts should be concerned both with what students need to know and with what they are able to do. Knowledge is part of being able to do, just as being able to do is part of knowledge.

This view of curriculum is tied directly to a major topic of discussion at the conference: textbooks and tests as curriculum. Following the directions in the teacher's manual of a basal reader or elementary English program is not compatible with the idea of a learner-centered curriculum. Commercial publishers can provide useful materials and suggestions for activities, but they cannot develop a learner-centered program for an individual school. A learner-centered language arts program must be created within particular communities of teachers and students.

The influence of textbooks on the language arts curriculum is perhaps most pervasive in the reading area. The curriculum proposed by the elementary strand called for a focus on children's literature in the teaching of reading. The elementary strand, like representatives from the other levels of schooling at the conference, felt that there should be no particular list of works that should be taught at particular levels in the elementary school. Rather, the content of the curriculum should consist of works that challenge students as readers, writers, and thinkers. The recommendation that the curriculum be literature-based implies significant changes in the texts in basal reading series. Because, especially at the beginning levels of such series, the language and content of basal readers are typically homogenized, formulaic, and simplified, children do not encounter vocabulary, syntax, or ideas that adequately prepare them to predict what they can expect in reading other texts. Furthermore, encounters with texts of this type can lead students to conceptualize reading as a process involving little more than literal understanding. The active reader responds personally, reads texts critically, interpretively, and aesthetically, and eventually develops to the point of understanding texts in terms of their historical and ideological contexts. Becoming an active reader of this sort begins with the child's earliest reading lessons. Clearly, because the school plays an important role in these early reading lessons, the materials of the curriculum are of great significance.

The curriculum must encourage children to read widely and in different ways. Teachers who follow all the recommendations for skill activities in the basal program or who judge children's progress by how many levels of the program they have read or how many end-of-unit tests they have passed are not having children read as broadly or as diversely as they should. Children's literature is not merely enrichment material for the language arts curriculum; it should be the foundation.

A major problem in the language arts curricula of many present-day elementary schools is a lack of integration, which occurs at both the "macro" and "micro" levels. Listening, speaking, reading, and writing should be part of every subject area in the elementary school, but often lessons in science or social studies are unrelated to language arts lessons. Even within the language arts, English and reading may be taught separately, or reading and writing instruction may not be correlated. At the most "micro" level it is not uncommon to find that skills lessons in the reading program or language arts workbook are unconnected with each other or with the reading selections or composition assignments.

Integration is a key characteristic of the elementary school curriculum proposed at the conference. In this curriculum, the study of writing is linked to the study of literature so that the "close relationship between composing meaning as we write and as we read" (Jensen 1984) can be capitalized on in the instructional program. Media studies are an integral part of English studies. The overall curriculum is content-oriented, or idea-oriented, instead of being driven by isolated skill work. One way of organizing this type of curriculum is through thematic planning, or webbing. For example, in a unit focused on flight, learners would read stories and informational books about flight, record results from science experiments on flight and draw conclusions about aerodynamic principles, measure flight distances, calculate flight equations, illustrate the concept of flight through creative movement, research some aspect of the history or future of flight, write imaginative stories or poems around a flight motif, and so forth. Such a curriculum promotes the development of knowledge and the interdisciplinary integration of information while it also promotes learning the skills of listening, speaking, reading, and writing. In this way the fragmentation so harmful to students' learning is overcome.

The fragmentation of the curriculum was also seen as intimately related to an increasing emphasis on testing in schools. The language arts—particularly reading, grammar and usage, and writing—are fundamental parts of the testing programs. As of 1985, thirty-eight states and the District of Columbia were conducting mandatory basic skills testing of students (Perry 1985). Virtually every school district also assesses children each year with a standardized achievement test that includes subtests on reading, vocabulary, spelling, capitalization and punctuation, and language usage. These tests tend to emphasize the separateness rather than the interrelatedness of the language arts. Ultimately, curriculum is affected because testing programs influence the way teachers teach. There is a tendency to "teach to" the tests (Frederiksen 1984; Lerner 1981).

The language arts curriculum should go hand in hand with an effective assessment program. However, it should be remembered that standardized tests are only a part of the well-designed assessment program and are generally more useful for looking at programs than at individuals. Individual assessment must be based on the principles and assumptions about learning that support the goals outlined earlier in this chapter and on the principles of curriculum integration proposed in this section. The ultimate aim of any assessment program is to provide optimal learning for all (Johnston 1987). In short, testing and teaching must be brought together. In order to accomplish this objective we must make assessment more like instruction. Information from structured performance samples and observations of the language learner must be legitimized in the assessment process. Instead of expanding current testing programs, we must spend money and invest our efforts in developing instruments and techniques that will help teachers to teach better in their classrooms.

In the late 1980s there are signs that this process is beginning. Authors are developing books like *Observing the Language Learner* (Jaggar and Smith-Burke 1985), which emphasizes nonstandardized alternatives in assessment; Michigan (Wixson, Peters, Weber and Roeber 1987) and Illinois (Valencia and Pearson 1986) have made strides in revamping elementary school basic skills testing; and North Carolina has passed legislation to replace standardized testing of reading and writing in first and second grades with informal, classroom-based assessment. Developments like these do bring testing and teaching closer together. Assessment is not incompatible with a learner-centered curriculum, but current assessment practices do not mesh well with optimal language arts instruction.

An effective language arts curriculum cannot be based on textbooks or tests. It must be centered on learners and formulated according to sound principles of child learning and sound theories of language and literacy acquisition.

Teaching English in the Elementary School

All of us have read reports about what the language arts curriculum or the teaching of English *should* be like. Frequently we come away from such reports with the feeling that, for the past decade at a minimum, the authors have not come within five miles of a public elementary school, much less worked with real children in a classroom setting. Either their recommendations are not put in terms applicable to the day-to-day life in classrooms, they are simply not realistic, or both. The members of the elementary strand at the conference were very concerned that "Language Arts for the 21st Century" not represent simply a pie-in-the-sky view of language arts education. If the gap between what is and what would be nice cannot be bridged, the report would look good on the book shelf but would be virtually useless to the elementary school personnel whose job it is to provide the best possible education for children.

From the outset our top priority was to include in our report specifics about how the goals and principles we envisioned for language arts instruction could be translated into the day-to-day activities of the classroom. We decided to provide a section entitled "A Look Inside the Elementary School Classroom." I present this section of the report here almost in its entirety because it provides information about classroom instruction and discusses issues of key importance in considering reform in the teaching of English in any school.

A Look Inside the Elementary Classroom

In this section of the report we tell our story about the kind of classroom in which language arts flourish and children are nurtured. We are mindful of the idealistic sound of this classroom, but we present the classroom as we know it can be. Classrooms like this do exist; some of them are ours. We teach and have taught in diverse situations—in cities and suburbs; with white, black, Latino, Native American, and Asian children; with "special needs" children and the "gifted and talented"—and we resist the notion that either the perceived problems of the children or of the teaching situation provide ready-made excuses to give in or to give up.

We recognize that there are serious problems to overcome. We have already written about some of the problems of today's children. Teachers, too, face myriad problems that mitigate against the kind of classrooms we describe:

- Teachers are not viewed by the public or school administrators as professionals. They are therefore treated like technicians, e.g., given "teacher-proof" materials, assigned nonprofessional duties.
- Curriculum is driven by textbooks and tests. In the name of accountability, teachers are asked to use graded texts with scripted workbooks. Test scores are used to sort children and to compare teachers and schools.
- Schools are financed by public monies. Often this means that change is resisted because the school budget is not large enough, which results in problems like large class size, a dearth of materials such as library books or even pencils and paper, or the unavailability of support personnel such as counselors or teacher aides.

We know that change must take place before the classroom we describe will be the norm in this country. Nevertheless we also know it can be done. In the Implications section of this report, we address the ways administrators, teacher educators, and policymakers can help to make it happen.

In looking at the elementary classroom, we consider four factors: (1) the child and the teacher, (2) the stuff of the classroom, (3) organization, and (4) climate.

The Child and the Teacher

The classroom is a community of learners. As in any community, its members assume roles as they spend time with each other. In the effective language arts classroom, teachers are in charge of their teaching and children are in charge of their learning. It is important to realize, however, that the role of teacher and the role of learner are intimately related, each defined in terms of the other.

The teacher is an expert and authority on learning and pedagogy, and in some subject matter fields as well. She is a researcher working both theoretically and practically. She is herself a skillful user of language—a reader and a writer as well as a speaker and listener. Even before the children enter the classroom, she plans, organizes, chooses materials, considers teaching strategies. She sets up a structured learning environment to ensure that the desired academic and social interactions are fostered. These activities become ongoing ones throughout the school year.

When the teacher works with the children, his role is delicately balanced between that of a manager/director and an enabler/interactor with them and their learning. Interactions involve individuals, small groups, or the whole class. As children read, write, talk, and listen, the teacher accepts and affirms their language. He also helps them extend and expand their language by having them use it—in all modes—to make meaning in all areas of the curriculum. The teacher provides information and direction. More often, he responds thoughtfully to children's efforts—with questions, statements, or even laughter and hugs. The teacher also models appropriate actions and attitudes by sharing his personal interests, his curiosity, his affection and respect for children. He also systematically observes children in informal ways in order to assess their progress toward desired ends.

Children bring to the classroom their language proficiency, their curiosity, their own learning styles, their sense of themselves as learners and as people, and their own special authority and expertise. They develop as active learners by participating in planned activities, thinking and questioning, creating, exploring, experimenting, making choices and decisions, and playing. In the process of acquiring knowledge and skill, children make mistakes that are valued as a part of learning. They become risk-takers as their discoveries and contributions are acknowledged and supported by other members of the classroom community. In an environment of trust and respect, sharing and collaborating between children and among children and adults are the norm.

Sometimes the roles that the teacher and children play are shared ones. Both the teacher and the children are responsible for being contributing members of the classroom community. Both are evaluators of their progress, sometimes finding reason to celebrate, sometimes finding a need to reconsider and reengage an experience. Both are thinkers. The teacher thinks about the teaching/learning interactions with the children and reflects on how and why. Children think about the experiences they engage in and reflect on their learning. Within the classroom community, both the teacher and the children are active learners.

The classroom community may also include adults other than the teacher. They may be parents, community volunteers, or specialists within the school such as librarians, art teachers, or reading specialists. Other students may also be invited in from time to time. Like the teacher, these helpers can interact with individuals, small groups, or the whole class, depending on the purpose of their involvement. Some may be information sources and role models; others may be listeners, readers, responders, or storytellers; still others may provide various kinds of support and support services such as funds for special projects or help in typing children's books. Making use of such adults extends the sense of community beyond the walls of the classroom and the school.

The Stuff of the Classroom

The selection and use of materials in an effective elementary classroom must be based on the characteristics of the children who will use them. The diversity of the children must be reflected in the variety of materials. Not only must the materials reflect the varying learning styles, language proficiencies, and interests of the children, they must be easily and always accessible. Despite the physical and fiscal constraints on room size, wall and floor treatments, and the amount and type of furniture, a classroom can be a child-centered one in which the organization, variety, and accessibility of materials entices and accommodates the child.

It is impossible to specify exactly what should be in a classroom to promote children's language and literacy development most effectively. Nevertheless, several key components are characteristic of classrooms with high quality language arts instruction.

Classroom Library. Classroom libraries model what we believe about books. The number and diversity of books, the authors included, the forms of text, all represent what we value as texts and what we value as prior knowledge that a child brings to text. What we exclude we devalue by omission.

Further, classroom libraries model what we believe about becoming lifelong readers. The number and diversity of ways in which children read, respond, get together, and share books—all are conducive to the development of a lifelong reader. The many ways that a classroom library can entice and engage a reader reflect what we believe about the act of reading. A classroom library that celebrates the diversity, backgrounds, interests, and potential of children includes:

- A generous ratio of books to students (a minimum of three to five books per student is recommended).
- Trade books representing a variety of genres, areas of interest, degrees of complexity (it is extremely important to include nonfiction texts along with stories).
- Books authored by children.
- Books authored by community members (other schoolchildren, friends, neighbors, family).

- Magazines and other periodicals.
- Book-related environmental print such as signs, labels, stickers, book covers, and posters.

Writing Materials and Media. A child's world is rich with a wide variety of writing materials and media: billboards, neon lights, food labels, menus, bumper stickers, tombstones, post-a-notes, birthday cards, and cucumber-shaped pens. The classroom environment can make a very important connection between school and the world outside the school by representing at least some of the diversity in writing materials and media that exists outside the school. This diversity can include:

- A variety of papers in different sizes, shapes, textures, and colors (including poster board, stationery).
- A variety of writing implements (including pencils, pens, crayons, novelty pens, felt-tip markers, a typewriter, a word processor).
- A variety of writing resources (including word lists, a thesaurus, spelling checkers, dictionaries).
- A variety of electronic expressive media (including tape recorders, record players, computers, camcorders, cameras, movie cameras).

Dramatic Expression and Play Area. The child's toys become the adult's tools. The roles the child plays become the ways of the adult. Many props can exist in the mind of a child, and dramatic arts are, in fact, performed without props. But without the space, the time, and the materials for dramatic expression and play, the child cannot rehearse the adult he or she will become. The classroom that values that rehearsal will have:

- Space for role-playing, dramatization, and improvisation.
- A variety of expressive media (including costumes, puppets, masks, makeup).
- A variety of props:
    - Appliances, furniture, store counters, transportation and building models, backgrounds, stage.
    - Costumes, masks, makeup.
    - Dolls and action figures, puppets.
    - Print props for a variety of dramatic play settings (e.g., appointment books, lists, tickets, bills, deposit slips).
- A variety of scripts, both print and nonprint, role-playing, improvisation, comedy, readers' theater.

Artistic Expression. During the developmental period, when children are translating concepts and thoughts into symbols, they need opportunities to choose from a variety of graphic as well as alphabetic and numeric forms. A diversity of media increases the possibilities for dialogue between child, picture, and word. Areas in which this dialogue can take place freely:

- Have a variety of media (including chalk, clay, watercolors, computer graphics).
- Provide opportunities to use artistic expression to complement or supplement language, or even as a catalyst for language.
- Are easy to clean up.

Multisensory Interaction. Children need physical interaction with animals, plants, and objects, and they need opportunities to probe and experiment—to hypothesize, and to test their hypotheses—about the relationships among these animals, plants, and objects. At some point, too, children need exposure to realistic and abstract representations; they need to compare and contrast these recreations with their real counterparts. The wider diversity of real and representative objects, the greater the child's understanding. Experiences that address all the senses may include:

- Artifacts.
- Live animals and plants.
- Preserved animals and plants.
- Tools for observation (including microscopes, thermometers, magnifying glasses, probes).
- Realistic and abstract representations of objects, animals, and plants for comparing and contrasting with real objects, animals, and plants (including artistic and musical representations, photographs, audio cassettes, films).
- Models (including true-to-size models, smaller- and larger-scale models)
- Collections.

Special Location for Keeping Student Work. A special location where children can keep their work serves many purposes, some as basic as contributing to a sense of organization. For many children, it is important simply to have a place that is wholly theirs. For others, having a central location for drafts and other writing can serve as a heuristic record, a way of seeing progress and direction in their language and thoughts. Student work locations are characterized by individual student areas (e.g., folder, drawer, box, tray) where the privacy of student work is respected.

Organization

Organization is the third important aspect of the effective elementary classroom. Appropriate allocation of time—uninterrupted blocks of time—is central to developing a classroom organization that allows for adequate planning and is conducive to learning. The allocation of time is stable yet flexible. Within a five-hour school day, extended blocks of time permit the teacher to weave the various aspects of the curriculum into a rich fabric. Naturally related subjects can be brought together in ways not possible within the forty- or fifty-minute framework predominant in secondary or departmentalized elementary schools. When teacher and children feel free to use time in a fluid and flexible way, they are able to become emotionally, intellectually, and creatively committed to the task at hand, thereby "uncovering" rather than covering curriculum; they are free to be spontaneous and to savor language and literature.

Grouping is another important facet of classroom organization. A flexible attitude toward grouping children allows a community to develop. Rather than establishing several firmly fixed reading groups based on ability and basal readers, the teacher can design a literature-based program that invites flexible patterns for grouping children. Whole group, small group, paired, or one-to-one meetings are based on children's interests, group dynamics, and personal needs. Interaction among all class members for various reasons and in a variety of settings is desirable. In this way, children can become personally invested in language learning.

Finally, the accessibility and use of materials contribute to the general tone and organization of a classroom. When a child has opportunities to choose materials, work in a variety of situations, and interact with all class members in an environment that is predictable but not static, exciting but not chaotic, and disciplined without being restrictive, the child is more likely to become a responsible and responsive member of a learning community.

Climate

Classroom climate relates closely to classroom organization. When teacher and children come together the first day of school, they begin to create a classroom climate. The perceptive teacher listens to children, observes the ways they learn, and finds a variety of strategies to engage them in learning, thus establishing a nurturing climate. Slowly and carefully, teacher and children build a predictable, yet fluid, structure within which there is a sense of order as well as freedom for exploration and open interaction. In this kind of climate teacher and children respect and value each other and continually shape a community in which individuals can flourish as well as participate as integral members of the group.

Crucial elements that contribute to the climate of the classroom include teachers' responses to children, the elements of trust and responsibility, and, once again, the use of time.

Responses. Teachers need to respond to children in ways that enable them to explore options, make choices, and participate in meaning-making experiences. Teachers not only bring their expertise and authority to interactions with children, but also nudge and question to stimulate thinking and to enable children to ask their own questions and seek answers.

Trust and Responsibility. Trust means valuing the learner as a human being who has much to give, demonstrate, and teach others. A trusted individual becomes a risk-taker, and to engage in learning is to engage in risk. Trust permits learners to take responsibility for and maintain ownership of their learning.

Time. Children need chunks of time each day to engage in language activities for real purposes. The pace of the classroom is determined partly in response to the development and interests of the child. Time is also devoted to play and reflection because these are valued aspects of learning and growth.

The nurturing classroom climate empowers all learners to seek meaning through reading, writing, listening, and talking and to be continually involved in active inquiry.

This look inside the elementary classroom has focused on particular characteristics of an effective environment for language arts instruction. It should also be obvious, however, that these characteristics have been described in general terms. Our intention was not to stop at this level of generality. The chapters that follow tell specific stories about classrooms. We hope that the combination of the general and the specific contained in this volume will provide a clear indication of the conception of effective language arts instruction proposed by the elementary representatives at the Coalition of English Associations Conference.

Thus far we have focused largely on classroom teachers. But teachers are not solely responsible for the education provided in the nation's elementary schools. The reform in language arts education cannot be accomplished without the cooperation of others who work with schools or whose policies directly influence schools.

Implications for School Administrators, Teacher Educators, and Policymakers

This section summarizes the implications of a learner-centered view of the teaching of English for school administrators, teacher educators, and policymakers at the local, state, and national levels. If the recommendations made in this report are to be realized, all of these groups must contribute to invigorating the teaching of English in the elementary school.

School Administrators
- School administrators will be learners who understand children's language growth because they:
  - Observe and listen to children in the classroom and throughout the school.
  - Talk regularly with teachers about their language arts goals and procedures.
  - Participate with teachers in districtwide in-service programs related to language.
  - Attend and participate in language-related sessions at meetings of professional associations for administrators.
  - Read and publish reports of exemplary administrative leadership of language arts programs.
- School administrators will support the ongoing learning of teachers and children by:
  - Joining with teachers and children in establishing a learning community.
  - Establishing a school professional library that contains materials reflecting current viewpoints about the teaching of language arts endorsed by professional organizations like The National Council of Teachers of English.
  - Providing time and encouragement for faculty groups to discuss issues and documents of professional concern.
  - Tapping the resources of professional associations like NCTE and the International Reading Association and their affiliates to enrich in-service education.
  - Encouraging teachers to participate in extended educational opportunities beyond the school (e.g., enroll in the National Writing Project, attend conventions of professional associations, participate

in summer institutes like those sponsored by the NEH, register for college courses) and reward them for participating.
- Encouraging teachers to observe the teaching of their colleagues.
- Making it possible for teachers to request demonstrations in their classrooms of aspects of language arts teaching.
- Coordinating efforts to communicate with parents about school language arts goals, instruction, and assessment procedures (e.g., through parent organizations like the PTA, through distribution of materials such as NCTE's "How to Help Your Child Become a Better Writer").
- Joining with teachers and parents in celebrating learning rather than grades and test scores; communicating with parents about their child's language growth in clear, informative, and theoretically sound ways.
- Enlisting the aid of the community at large in supporting the school language arts program (e.g., recruiting volunteer aids, developing business contacts, finding ways for citizens to serve as resource persons in the classroom, compiling a directory of places where teachers can take children to learn outside the school).

Teacher Educators
- Teacher educators will design theoretically sound programs that:
  - View teaching as art as well as science.
  - Develop in future teachers a sense of purpose, belief, and commitment to the profession that will serve as a rationale for their behavior.
  - Integrate language-related courses, rather than enrolling students in separate courses for reading methods, language arts methods, and children's literature.
  - Are staffed by faculty who know not only about subject matter but about children and their language learning (e.g., children's literature professors should know not only books, but the nature of the interactions that may take place between a book and a child).
  - Equip future teachers to reflect and to adopt a reflective practitioner perspective (i.e., a teacher-researcher perspective) on students' learning and their own teaching.
- Teacher educators will negotiate with elementary school personnel the methods for achieving goals so that:
  - Future teachers receive support from both the college or university supervisor and the cooperating teacher.

- Those cooperating teachers will be the finest possible classroom models (possibly on the faculties of "key" or demonstration schools).
- Teacher educators will work with college and university administrators in an effort to support a reward structure that values school involvement by faculty.
- Teacher educators will encourage collaborative research between teacher educators and classroom teachers.

Policymakers

Policy decisions will be informed by the principles of language learning and teaching outlined in this report. Accordingly, legislators, school board members, employees of state and federal agencies, and others will seek the advice of English language arts professionals and their organizations as they:

- Adopt or design instruments for assessing literacy.
- Determine the uses of assessment data.
- Set priorities for the granting of funds for language-related research (see the research priorities outlined in the following section).
- Make budgetary decisions related to language arts curriculum and teaching (e.g., class size, professional growth opportunities).

Three forces for improving the quality of language arts education for elementary school children are school administrators who are themselves learners and who support the learning of both teachers and children, teacher educators who design theoretically sound programs and who implement them in collaboration with positive classroom models, and policymakers whose decisions rest on sound professional advice.

Research Priorities

Sound educational programs always grow out of a research base. Therefore, the final section of the report presented recommendations for research we believed especially important to pursue at this time if the principles of language learning and the practices of language arts teaching embodied in the report were to become widespread in the schools of America. Some of the recommendations apply to all levels of schooling;

others are priorities specifically geared to the elementary school. In either case they play an important part in the elementary report because we believed so strongly that research and instruction must continue to inform each other. The research priorities recommended include:

- Studies of the textual materials used in the teaching of reading, with special attention to the role of children's literature.
- Content analyses of the extent to which graded language arts, spelling, and handwriting textbooks reflect the principles of language learning and teaching embodied in this report.
- Studies of the effects of self-contained vs. departmentalized elementary classroom organization on language arts teaching and student achievement that identify trends and make recommendations.
- Studies of the effects of models for teaching writing used by the National Writing Project on student achievement in writing and teaching practices at the elementary level.
- Evaluations of the efficacy of applying the principles exemplified by the National Writing Project to the teaching of literature.
- Case studies of outstanding classrooms in which the teaching of language arts reflects the principles embodied in this report. Especially important will be identification of the factors that have encouraged their development and sustained their growth.
- Studies of why elementary language arts teachers teach the way they do (e.g., Do they show principled behavior? How are their instructional decisions affected by external conditions such as legislation, school district policies, building administrators?).
- Case studies of effective administrative models for developing exemplary elementary language arts programs.
- Studies of the ways in which computers contribute to students' language learning in classrooms that embody the principles stated in this report.
- Examinations of the role of teacher support groups in establishing and maintaining theory-driven practice in language arts instruction.
- Studies of the effects of censorship on the literary experiences of elementary school children.
- Descriptive studies of children's engagement with oral language, reading, and writing during the elementary school day.
- Studies of the development of effective home–school cooperation in the achievement of language arts objectives, with special attention to difficult-to-reach families.
- Studies of the effects of television programming related to the language arts (e.g., "Reading Rainbow," "Sesame Street").
- Studies of effective means of disseminating models of classroom practice

that adhere to the principles outlined in this report (e.g., print, video, conferences, institutes, classroom demonstrations).
- Setting of standards for the development of measurement instruments consistent with the principles outlined in this report. Especially deserving of investigation are informal and observational instruments useful to teachers in making instructional decisions.
- Developing collaborative models for pre-service and in-service language arts teacher education, beginning with a national conference that will bring together educators from a range of disciplines and school levels.

It is important to note that the research priorities outlined here can be accomplished only when such studies are informed by ongoing inquiry into the nature of language processes. Ever-increasing understanding of the acts of reading and writing, the relationships between reading and writing, the acquisition of oral language, and the nature of language growth is the foundation for studies like those above. One belief universally echoed in the Coalition Conference was the interrelation of theory and practice in teaching. Therefore, it is imperative that a major commitment to basic research on language and language learning accompany these priorities.

A Look Back; A Look Forward

The Coalition of English Associations Conference was intended to promote discussion about the teaching of English in American schools by describing current theoretical and practical conceptions in the field and recommending directions the field should take in the coming decades. Now that the perspective of the elementary strand on these issues has been presented, it seems fitting to step back from the report to gain a perspective on what has been recommended. To do so, I should like to take a backward look at the last invitational seminar of this type, the Anglo-American Conference on the Teaching of English of 1966, or the Dartmouth seminar, as it has come to be called. This retrospective look can help us to understand what is new, what is different, and what is not so new and different in the current report. In other words, it can suggest the directions we have taken in English education. It can also enable us to engage in a bit of soothsaying, to speculate on what effects the present report may have upon language arts theory and practice during the coming two decades.

Dartmouth and the Aspen Coalition Conference

In retrospect, it is clear that the Dartmouth seminar significantly affected conceptions and methods of English teaching in the United States. The major force at the conference was the group of British educators who brought with them ideas about English curriculum and activities quite different from those prevailing in the United States at the time. The Dartmouth conference and follow-up visitations by teams of American educators to forty-two British schools during the spring of 1967 caused many Americans to change their minds about the teaching of English (Squire and Applebee 1969). While concern for literary heritage and knowledge of the academic model of literary criticism dominated the American English curriculum, the British offered a model for English studies based on the personal and linguistic growth of the child rather than on the "demands" of the discipline (Applebee 1974). This model considered personal experience the vital core of work in English (Dixon 1967), and focused on process rather than content. An emphasis on a thematic approach to curriculum, stressing response to literature through talking about it, attention to the act of writing itself, and the use of drama in teaching were hallmarks of the British approach (Dixon 1967; Muller 1967). Although the use of drama has never caught on in American schools in the way it was used in British schools, it is possible to see the influence of the other characteristics of the British model on the English curriculum in American schools throughout the 1970s and 1980s.

Having read the report contained in the present chapter, one might legitimately ask, "How have ideas changed or not changed since Dartmouth?" At one level "Language Arts for the 21st Century" may sound very familiar. Much like the models that emerged from Dartmouth, we stressed the need for the curriculum to be learner-centered. Decisions about goals, activities, and materials should stem from consideration of the individuals being taught, not merely from some predetermined notion of what should be covered in the curriculum or from some abstract list of what constitutes the skills of English. The elementary report represents a belief that we teach children English, not that we teach English.

But unlike the message that emanated from Dartmouth, we hope that our concern for content as well as for process comes through. Though we eschewed the notion of a list of specific works that should be taught at a particular level, we greatly stressed the importance of the types of texts students read. Perhaps it was because there were so few representatives at Dartmouth with elementary school teaching experience (and no one there who was at the time teaching in an American school below the secondary level) that the issue of the nature of materials used in the elementary classroom did not seem to come up. In contrast, the Coalition Conference could be described as almost preoccupied by what students were reading during their Reading and English time in the classroom. Discussions about basal readers and children's literature continued from the beginning of the three-week period to the end. The recommendation for a literature-based curriculum was unanimous. The concern that the content of the curriculum should be texts (both narrative and expository) that challenge students as readers, writers, and thinkers was equally strong. Thus, the issue of content was put on equal footing with the issue of process. There was a recognition that a sound English program paid considerable attention to what students were reading and learning. In this sense, Aspen brought more of a balance to the recommendations for the teaching of English: both process and content were considered to be of extreme importance in building a strong curriculum.

In several respects the recommendations from the Coalition Conference extend those made twenty years ago. Dartmouth called for a thematic center to instruction in English. The elementary strand echoed that stance but also extended it in significant ways; perhaps the most important are attempts like those in the remaining chapters in this book to tell stories about how such a curriculum works in reality. Again, I think the presence of so many classroom teachers at the Coalition meeting moved the group in this direction. It was not good enough to talk about a curriculum; the group attempted to demonstrate what was being espoused by providing specific pictures and stories of effective language arts classrooms.

A second major emphasis at the Coalition Conference that extended work from the Dartmouth seminar was in the area of multiculturalism and English studies. At Dartmouth, attention seemed to focus on "the disadvantaged," many of whom happened to be ethnic minorities and speakers of nonstandard dialect or of English as a second language. The issue of students at risk of failure in American schools is every bit as prevalent today as it was twenty years ago. However, the Coalition Conference approach to matters about nonmainstream children and multiculturalism seemed different. In a sense the topic pervaded discussions from start to finish, but although it was specifically the focus of attention at particular times, it was not a special topic dealt with for an hour here or an afternoon there. In addition, cultural diversity was not addressed as a problem to be dealt with but as a resource to be cultivated. The topic of the content of English studies was also very much a part of discussions that touched on multiculturalism. Participants at all levels of schooling stressed the need for students to read texts representing a variety of cultural and ideological perspectives. A strong line of research has also developed, over the past ten to fifteen years especially, that takes a sociocultural perspective on language and literacy development (see, for example, the work of Heath 1983; or the review of sociolinguistic studies in reading by Bloome and Green 1984). Results from research like this have helped to place social and cultural issues in the center of discussions about English studies rather than separating them out as a specialized topic. Thus, it might be said that we as a profession have come of age in addressing the issue of multiculturalism in the teaching of English. Perhaps I am being too optimistic, but I believe that the goals proposed by the elementary strand indicate that we have entered an era in which sociocultural factors feature prominently in the curriculum and practices of the elementary school.

Other extensions of ideas generated at Dartmouth have resulted from the tremendous amount we have learned from the past two decades of research in language and literacy acquisition and in the teaching of English. At one point in *Growth through English*, John Dixon says, "In the pre-school years, almost all children miraculously acquire [language]" (Dixon 1967, 30). It may have seemed like a miracle twenty years ago to educators feeling the emerging influence of Chomsky's theory. But thanks to the diligent and far-reaching work of scholars in fields like anthropology, education, linguistics, psychology, sociology, philosophy of language, rhetoric, semiotics, and artificial intelligence, language and literacy learning is not as much of a black box. For example, we have made great strides in understanding the writing process, an idea that was only nascent in the Dartmouth reports. We have gained additional insights into response to literature and have attempted to incorporate these into the teaching of reading in the elementary school. In short, we know more now than we did then, and the recommendations about students, about curriculum, and about classroom practices are stronger for it.

There are differences between the Dartmouth and Coalition conferences as well. Some issues that predominated at Dartmouth—the use of drama or the issue of dialect, for example—attracted relatively little attention at Aspen. In the case of dialect, I think the comparative lack of attention can also be linked to the research findings of recent years. We clearly have not solved the issue of dialect and English and reading instruction in our schools, but research has clearly indicated what we *ought* to be doing. (Now we just have to do it.) On the other hand, a topic like testing received a scant three pages of discussion in Dixon's (1967) book but pervaded the entire Coalition Conference. This difference can be traced to the growth of achievement and competency testing in the United States over the past two decades. It also relates to the increasingly predominant role that testing plays in shaping instructional materials and methods. Testing has become the enemy of a learner-centered curriculum because this type of assessment runs counter to the approach to teaching supported by recent research in reading and writing. The elementary strand recommended revising the relationship so that assessment and teaching might be more closely linked.

Thus, the conclusions from the Coalition of English Associations Conference are not merely rehashings of ideas from Dartmouth, though they do clearly build on the foundation laid some twenty years ago. At the same time, the Coalition Conference recommendations also provide some new directions for the field to consider. Perhaps chief among these is the goal of having students become language theorists. Conferees were greatly influenced by Shirley Brice Heath's address at Aspen, in which she stressed the significant role that having students become "ethnographers," aware of the uses of language and literacy in their homes and communities, played in the success of her elementary and secondary school projects in Carolina and Alabama (Heath 1983; Heath and Branscombe 1985). Such an emphasis corresponds with conclusions from recent work on metacognition and metalinguistics showing that students who are good language users, readers, and writers are able to monitor and adjust their language and literacy strategies. This focus on the importance of having students become language theorists represents a new emphasis for the English curriculum. In fact, this may be a profitable way for the study of language to be realized in the curriculum, thereby avoiding the negative aspects of grammar study that have plagued the profession for so long.

A second significant emphasis in the elementary strand recommendations is the high priority placed on students' being readers and writers, and it is no accident that this goal is the first in the list presented earlier. The Coalition recommendations about curriculum and classroom practices reflect the importance of fostering voluntary reading and writing habits in children. Although the goal is certainly not a new one for the teaching of English, we chose to make it explicit and primary, for we believed that it is the foundation on which successful language arts learning and teaching rests.

A third development that resulted from the Coalition Conference is that the concept of reflective practitioner, or teacher-researcher, has come into its own. Good teachers continuously reflect upon what they are doing in the classroom. Their instructional programs are informed by sound research in language and literacy learning and teaching. Their classrooms are research laboratories in which they instruct and modify instruction to make it better. They use resources available from commercial publishers, but a published program is not their curriculum. Actually, the concept of reflective practitioner relates closely to the idea of students as language theorists. Reflective practitioners have the knowledge and the strategies to make their teaching an activity they continuously modify to make it better and better. This notion has profound implications for teacher education. If we are to help individuals develop into good teachers, we must plan pre-service and in-service programs that guide them to becoming reflective practitioners.

Finally, a distinctive characteristic of the Coalition Conference was the voice of the classroom teacher, which I have already mentioned in several places throughout the chapter. Let me add here that the nature of this book and of the conference overall were profoundly affected by individuals who work with children every day.

A Look Forward

I do not pretend to predict the future about the effect of the Coalition of English Associations Conference in general or the perspective taken by the elementary strand on the field of English. If Dartmouth is any indication, the ideas will at least stimulate discussion at a variety of levels about teaching, research, teacher education, and policy. For those of us who attended, the conference was a rare opportunity to think deeply about the teaching of English in American schools with a group of very knowledgeable people. It caused us to articulate what we know, what we don't know, and what we would like to know about the learning and teaching of oral and written language. I believe that the ideas proposed in "Language Arts for the 21st Century: The Crossroads of Possibility and Practice" represent a synthesis of significant advances in the field of elementary English studies. They also represent achievable advances. The real work comes in realizing these ideas daily in our classrooms, and that is what the remainder of this volume is about.

REFERENCES

Applebee, A. N. 1974. *Tradition and Reform in the Teaching of English: A History*. Urbana, Ill.: National Council of Teachers of English.

Bloome, D., and J. Green. 1984. "Directions in the Sociolinguistic Study of

Reading." In *Handbook of Reading Research*, ed. P. D. Pearson. New York: Longman.

Bruner, J. S. 1977. *The Process of Education*. 2d ed. Cambridge, Mass.: Harvard University Press.

——— 1983. *Child's Talk*. New York: Norton.

——— 1986. *Actual Minds, Possible Worlds*. Cambridge, Mass.: Harvard University Press.

Dewey, J. 1916. *Democracy and Education*. New York: Macmillan.

——— 1963. *Experience and Education*. New York: Collier.

Dixon, J. 1967. *Growth through English*. Reading, England: National Association for the Teaching of English.

Frederiksen, N. 1984. "The Real Test Bias." *American Psychologist* 39: 193–202.

Hawkins, D. 1979. "The Enlargement of the Esthetic." *Outlook* 34: 28–39.

Heath, S. B. 1983. *Ways with Words: Language, Life and Work in Communities and Classrooms*. Cambridge: Cambridge University Press.

Heath, S. B., and A. Branscombe. 1985. "Intelligent Writing in an Audience Community: Teacher, Students, and Researcher." In *The Acquisition of Written Language: Revision and Response*, ed. S. W. Freedman. Norwood, N.J.: Ablex.

Hirsch, E. D., Jr. 1987. *Cultural Literacy: What Every American Needs to Know*. Boston: Houghton Mifflin.

Jaggar, A., and M. T. Smith-Burke. 1985. *Observing the Language Learner*. Newark, Del. and Urbana, Ill.: International Reading Association and National Council of Teachers of English.

Jensen, J. M. 1984. *Composing and Comprehending*. Urbana, Ill.: National Conference on Research in English/ERIC Clearinghouse on Reading and Communication Skills.

Johnston, P. 1987. "Assessing the Process, and the Process of Assessment, in the Language Arts." In *The Dynamics of Language Learning*, ed. J. Squire, 335–57. Urbana, Ill.: National Conference on Research in English/ERIC Clearinghouse on Reading and Communication Skills.

Lerner, B. 1981. "The Minimum Competency Testing Movement: Social, Scientific, and Legal Implications." *American Psychologist* 36: 1057–66.

Muller, H. J. 1967. *The Uses of English*. New York: Holt, Rinehart & Winston.

Perry, K. M. 1985. *State-Mandated Assessment Programs: An Examination of the Issues*. Stillwater, Okla.: Oklahoma State University School of Education. (ERIC Document Reproduction Service No. ED 275 754).

Piaget, J. 1926. *The Language and Thought of the Child*. London: Routledge & Kegan Paul.

——— 1983. "Piaget's Theory." In *Handbook of Child Psychology*, ed. P. H.

Mussen. *Vol. 1, History, Theory and Methods*, ed. W. Kessen. New York: John Wiley & Sons.

Squire, J. R., and R. K. Applebee. 1969. *Teaching English in the United Kingdom*. Urbana, Ill.: National Council of Teachers of English.

Valencia, S. W., and P. D. Pearson. 1986. *Reading Assessment Initiative in the State of Illinois, 1985–86*. Springfield, Ill.: Illinois State Board of Education.

Vygotsky, L. S. 1978. *Mind in Society*. Cambridge, Mass.: Harvard University Press.

——— 1986. *Thought and Language*. Cambridge, Mass.: MIT Press.

Wixson, K., C. Peters, E. Weber, and D. Roeber. 1987. "New Directions in Statewide Reading Assessment." *The Reading Teacher* 40: 749–54.

TEACHERS TELLING THEIR STORIES

part II

*...whatever its subject matter,
every story is about change. This change
must be important to the hero,
for if it doesn't matter to him or her,
the reader will not care.*
—*Uri Shulevitz*
Writing with Pictures

2

From the First

Teaching to Diversity

CAROL S. AVERY

Early morning sunlight brightens the first-grade classroom. In many ways this is a traditional room: a chalkboard across the front, cinderblock walls painted yellow and orange, small student desks and one large teacher desk, a sink, a carpet in one corner, windows along one wall with shelves under them.

Today is the first day of school. The bulletin boards stand empty waiting for the children's ideas, and hundreds of books fill the shelves, chalkrails, table tops, and every available nook. The books represent a curriculum with children's literature as its foundation and the needs of children at its heart.

In this first-grade classroom, the basal reader is no longer used to teach reading. Language skills develop as children write, read, listen to literature read aloud, and talk with each other. Once curriculum-driven and teacher-centered, the classroom is now child-centered, with a learning environment that responds to, and capitalizes on, the variety of learning

Classroom libraries model what we believe about books.

styles and diversity of backgrounds of individual children. As the teacher in this room, I attempt to be a coach who responds to children's individual learning processes rather than a director who manages countless dittos and workbooks, prescribed lessons, and sequenced skills. I strive to make my classroom a *literate environment,* which Nancie Atwell (1985) says occurs in schools "wherever written language is the natural domain of the children and adults who work and play there."

The Way It Used to Be

In past years, preparing the classroom was a major project during the last weeks of summer. I created colorful bulletin boards, hung and mounted an assortment of hand-constructed, laminated figures, posters, and book jackets, and filled every inch of available display space. Administrators, parents, and fellow teachers told me that the room looked beautiful. No child ever commented on it. The only display the children demonstrated much interest in was the fifteen-inch-high strip that ran along the top of the chalkboard where each child's name was mounted. The children liked to read their names and referred to them when writing personal notes to one another. When the basal reader dominated the language curriculum, I managed three, sometimes four, reading groups a day. I planned creative seatwork and presented programmed lessons that fit into an exact spot on the scope and sequence chart. The curriculum and the directed lessons allowed little room for individual differences among children as readers.

During the last months of the school year, after the children could read, I allowed them to write. We produced beautiful class books. The children illustrated sentences they dictated while I wrote the words (so they would be correctly spelled, of course). One such book was *Our Dinosaur Book* by Room 3. They loved it—the pictures, that is. Few students bothered to read the words. On another occasion we popped popcorn with the lid off the popper. While popcorn flew like exploding fireworks across the front of the room, I raced to write on the chalkboard all of the descriptive words the children called out. Then they wrote one- or two-sentence "stories." Naturally, since all had the same experience and shared the same vocabulary, their stories sounded very much alike.

Occasionally, the children wrote by completing *story-starters*. When we studied dinosaurs they wrote stories that began "My pet dinosaur...." After I read *The March Wind* by Inez Rice, everyone wrote "If I wore the hat of the March wind...." The children's writing was bland and brief, and some children had difficulty in finding an idea to complete my directed assignment. An exception was the story-starter I used year after year, "When I was little...." Every child was able to come up with a memory from preschool years. Family stories told to the children time and again provided the material for their writing. The familiar content made the writing comfortable and meaningful. The children enjoyed writing and loved sharing these personal narratives.

The most enjoyable part of teaching, however, was the time I spent reading aloud to the class. As a former elementary librarian, I knew children loved to listen to stories, and I enjoyed responding to books with them, hearing their ideas, marveling at their insights. Incorporating read-aloud times into the first-grade schedule was natural. We read children's novels to begin the school day and picture books in the afternoon, and discovered nonfiction books to enhance science and social studies units. But despite my good intentions, a crowded schedule often shoved this time with children's books aside.

Then, in the late seventies, *Language Arts* began to report the research of Donald Graves on the writing processes of young children (1978–81a). Reading these articles, I found myself saying, "My kids can do that." I implemented some of the strategies for teaching writing that Graves and his colleagues reported and watched the ways the children in my classroom responded. The children's lively interest in writing and the energy that writing uncapped in the classroom spurred me to deeper involvement. I attended writing workshops, examined the ways I taught and the ways children learned, and searched out the latest research on children's language learning. As I read Graves, Atwell, Bissex, Calkins, Giacobbe, Harste, and others, I wrote to reflect and to make connections between research reports and my own classroom situation. Gradually, I learned to let go of control of the classroom, to share that control with the children, and to enter into a new type of teaching/learning relationship with my students.

The Way It Is Now

In the classroom today, my first graders and I function as teachers and learners in an environment that is rich with language. Every day we read a wide range of materials, write about real experiences for a variety of audiences and purposes, and listen to and share responses to literature.

As with any effective classroom environment, careful planning and implementation are required to build a community that can work, play, and learn together.

Each day students have a writing workshop, a reading workshop, and a literature time. During the writing and reading workshops, the children write on topics and read books of their own choosing. They receive responses from me and from each other while they are in the process of writing and reading. They learn to revise and edit their writing in order to clearly communicate meaning. They publish pieces they select as their best in correctly typed, wallpaper-covered books. During the literature time, they listen to children's literature read aloud, talk about their responses to the texts, and engage in various activities such as drama, puppetry, and art to express and extend their understandings of the stories. They use the components of language—reading, writing, listening, talking—for real purposes and real audiences, thus continuing their natural capacity for learning. As they collaborate, they glean ideas, insights, and strategies from others. The children learn from each other and develop an appreciation of their differences.

On the first morning of this new school year, I will begin by establishing procedures for writing and reading workshops and for literature time. As the day begins, the children are only names on a list, but by the time they walk out the door in the afternoon, I know something about their individual personalities. The comments the children make in response to the books we read, their first writing efforts, and the ways in which they approach books and reading tell me much about each child.

Sharing Children's Literature

The children and I begin our first hour of school on the carpet in the corner of the classroom. We chat informally and introduce ourselves; then I tell them about some of the things we will do this year. "Every day we will sit here and listen to stories," I say. Twenty-four faces light up. "Sometimes I'll read and sometimes you'll read. And we'll talk about what we read—what we feel or what the stories make us think about. But we'll do it every day."

As I open Marcia Brown's illustrated version of *The Three Billy Goats Gruff*, some children say, "Oh, I know *that* story!" or "It's a good one!" I read through the book, tapping my knuckles on the bench as the billy goats trip-trap across the bridge, and several children begin to tap the bookcase and the floor along with me. When I finish, they cry, "Read it again." I read it again and this time some chime in with the trip-traps and the ugly troll's roar, "Who's that tripping over my bridge?" I notice that Johnson, our Chinese boy, who speaks only a few words of English, watches the other children as well as the pictures in the book and taps his knuckles with them. Upon hearing the troll's roar, he giggles in delight.

When I close the book Dustin says, "I like that troll. He's funny!"

"Do you all think he's funny?" I ask.

"No!" says Meghan. "I think he's scary."

"He's like a monster," says Randy.

"Sorta like Halloween monsters," says Ben.

"When my brother was a monster at Halloween, *he* was scary, but then after I got used to him, he was funny," comments Carolyn.

"The big billy goat wasn't scared of the troll and the little one tricked him. I liked that he tricked him," says Oliver.

The children relax and drop their initial shyness and reserve. The talk about the story continues for several minutes. Some children participate in the conversation by voicing their ideas, while others listen and display their interest through nods, smiles, and giggles. The responses of the children grow both from their literal comprehension of the text, and from personal experiences. As they talk, each child's comments prompt further ideas in other children. Their ideas differ, but by sharing they expand their understandings of the story and make new connections. They learn together.

After a few minutes I introduce Eric Carle's *The Very Hungry Caterpillar* by asking the children what they know about caterpillars. Most understand the metamorphosis of caterpillars to butterflies, and many report catching caterpillars in jars or cans. We talk briefly about the role of an author in creating a book. I introduce Eric Carle as the author of this book and then we read.

The Very Hungry Caterpillar is new to many in the class. They enjoy the repetitious language—"but he was still hungry"—and the food the caterpillar devours. Cries of "Yum!" come from many as the story unfolds. They do not relate to the caterpillar's feeling better after eating one nice green leaf, but are still enthralled with all the tasty, rich foods he consumed earlier. This, I realize, is my reading of the story. Another day I will tell them my response, but not now. Sharing my ideas too early could stifle some of theirs and be interpreted as the "right" answer. I want them to understand that there is no one correct reading of a text, that we all bring our own ideas and experiences to a piece of literature, and that we can grow in our understanding of the text, and of each other, by listening to and sharing those ideas.

Children bring to the classroom their language proficiency, their curiosity, their own learning styles, their sense of themselves as learners and as people, and their own special authority and expertise.

Before putting this book aside, we look again at the illustrations, noting the holes in the pages that indicate where the caterpillar ate, and talking about the varying page sizes. Why did Mr. Carle make the book this way? The children think, speculate, and share a variety of ideas—all affirmed.

I conclude the literature time by reading a few nursery rhymes. Surprisingly, many children in the class are unfamiliar with them. In the days to come, we will chant them and clap their rhythms as we line up to go to art or gym. Nursery rhymes open the door for poetry reading and appreciation. Eventually, these first graders will become familiar with the works of many children's poets and selected poems of renowned poets such as Robert Frost and William Carlos Williams.

We will come back to this rug and read and talk together two more times before the first day is through. We will reread *The Very Hungry Caterpillar*, dramatize *The Three Billy Goats Gruff* with stick puppets, and discover several new books. The children will carry home caterpillars they make from half an egg carton, and I hope they will talk about the story with their families this evening.

Our daily literature time exposes us to a variety of children's books and authors throughout the year. We talk about the lives and writing of many authors, locate their pictures in the library, and add them to a bulletin board collection. The children's published books also become part of the classroom library, to be read during our daily time with literature. Tomorrow I will begin reading *Charlotte's Web* to them, one of a dozen novels we will enjoy this year. Interacting with children's literature will be a significant part of every school day.

Beginning Writing Workshop

Later on this first morning we begin our writing workshop. Because I want to respond individually to each child during the initial writing activity, I select five or six members of the class to meet with me at a round table. The others will work on a ditto—one of the few I will use throughout the year—at their seats. The paper requires little thought; I want them to eavesdrop on the conversations during the writing activity at the table.

I ask the children at the table to draw a picture of something they like or something important to them. During the drawing I speak with each child, encouraging talk about the experiences represented in the drawings. The work of Donald Graves has taught me the importance of developing student ownership of writing by listening, telling the child my understanding of what has been said, and asking questions to help the child expand and clarify ideas. When listening, I look at the writer, not at the writing, and try to maintain as much eye contact as possible, which demonstrates my interest in the child, not the product, and develops trust for risk-taking (Graves 1983).

The children open their crayon boxes. Danny spills the contents of his box on the table, looks through the colors, and selects a blue crayon. He swings the bright color across the bottom of his paper and a jagged line appears.

"Tell me about this, Danny," I say.

"Oh, this is the bay," he replies.

"The bay?" I ask.

"Yeah, the Chesapeake. The *Chesapeake* Bay. You know."

"Right, I know. The *Chesapeake* Bay. You've been there?"

"Well, that's where we keep our boat and that's where we go boating and crabbing and stuff."

"You keep your boat at the Chesapeake and go boating and crabbing. Well, how do you go crabbing? I mean, I *love* crabs but I don't know anything about crabbing."

Danny turns away from his picture to look at me. "Didn't you ever catch a crab before?" he asks.

"Never. How do you catch them?"

"Well, you can do it two ways." Danny's voice takes on an authoritative tone and he puts up one finger as he begins to explain. "One way is to just use a string and chicken neck from the side of the dock." A second finger goes up. "And the other way is with a trap. When my Dad and I go crabbing, *we* use a trap."

"So you can catch crabs two ways," I say, "with a chicken neck and string or with a trap. But *you* use a trap."

"Yeah," Danny replies as he turns back to his picture. "We go crabbing a lot and we go boating too."

"Thank you, Danny," I say and, noticing he has begun drawing again, I move on.

Across the table Trevor is drawing a dinosaur picture. I move around and stoop down beside him. "What's this about?"

"Dinosaurs," he replies. His lips purse and he presses hard with the crayon.

"Dinosaurs?"

The elementary report represents a belief that we teach children English, not that we teach English.

"Yeah, dinosaurs. I know a *lot* about dinosaurs. See, I can *read*." Trevor turns to look at me. "I like to read about dinosaurs." I nod. Before I can respond further, Trevor returns to his paper and continues drawing.

Jan has been sitting watching and listening. Her paper remains blank. "I don't know nothing to draw," she says as I approach her.

"Nothing? You know *nothing*?" I respond with mock amazement that brings a grin from Jan.

"Well, I do. But I just can't *think*," she replies.

"I see. Well, maybe you can think of something you really like, something you did that you'd like to do again?" I nudge.

For a moment Jan is pensive. "I like that caterpillar book you read us," she says. I wait. We exchange smiles and then Jan picks up a red crayon and turns to her paper.

I continue listening and responding to the children at the table. Each time I come near Danny he is eager to tell me more about his activities on the Chesapeake. "Danny," I say after he finishes telling me about the importance of running the motorboat through the channel, "you really know a lot about crabbing and boating and channels. I wonder, could you write some of those things here on the paper with your picture?"

Danny shakes his head. "I can't spell," he says.

"That's okay," I tell him, "A lot of grown-ups who have gone to school a long time can't spell either. And writers don't always spell correctly when they start to write. They fix it later. All you have to do is say the words you want to write slowly, listen for the letters, and write what you hear." With this assurance, Danny is willing to try.

All of the children conclude their time at the table by writing about their drawings. They produce a variety of results.

Jan draws orange, red, and purple circles and pencils a self-portrait (Figure 2–1). She labels them "O" for orange, "A" for apple, "P" for plum, and "ME." *The Very Hungry Caterpillar* provides Jan with her ideas. She draws easily but is unsure when I ask her to write. I acknowledge each letter she pencils on the paper with smiles and comments: "A—apple! O—orange! How do you know that?" "I seen them in my alphabet book at home," she replies.

Danny draws a simple sailboat (Figure 2–2) after talking at great length about his family's summer activities on the Chesapeake Bay. He knows about crabbing, harbors, channels, life jackets, and driving a boat. When he finishes the picture, he writes the words most important to him: life jacket. Danny tells about his experiences easily. When he writes he turns to me after each letter and asks, "Is that right?" "What do you think?" I ask. "I think it's right," he says and continues.

From the First

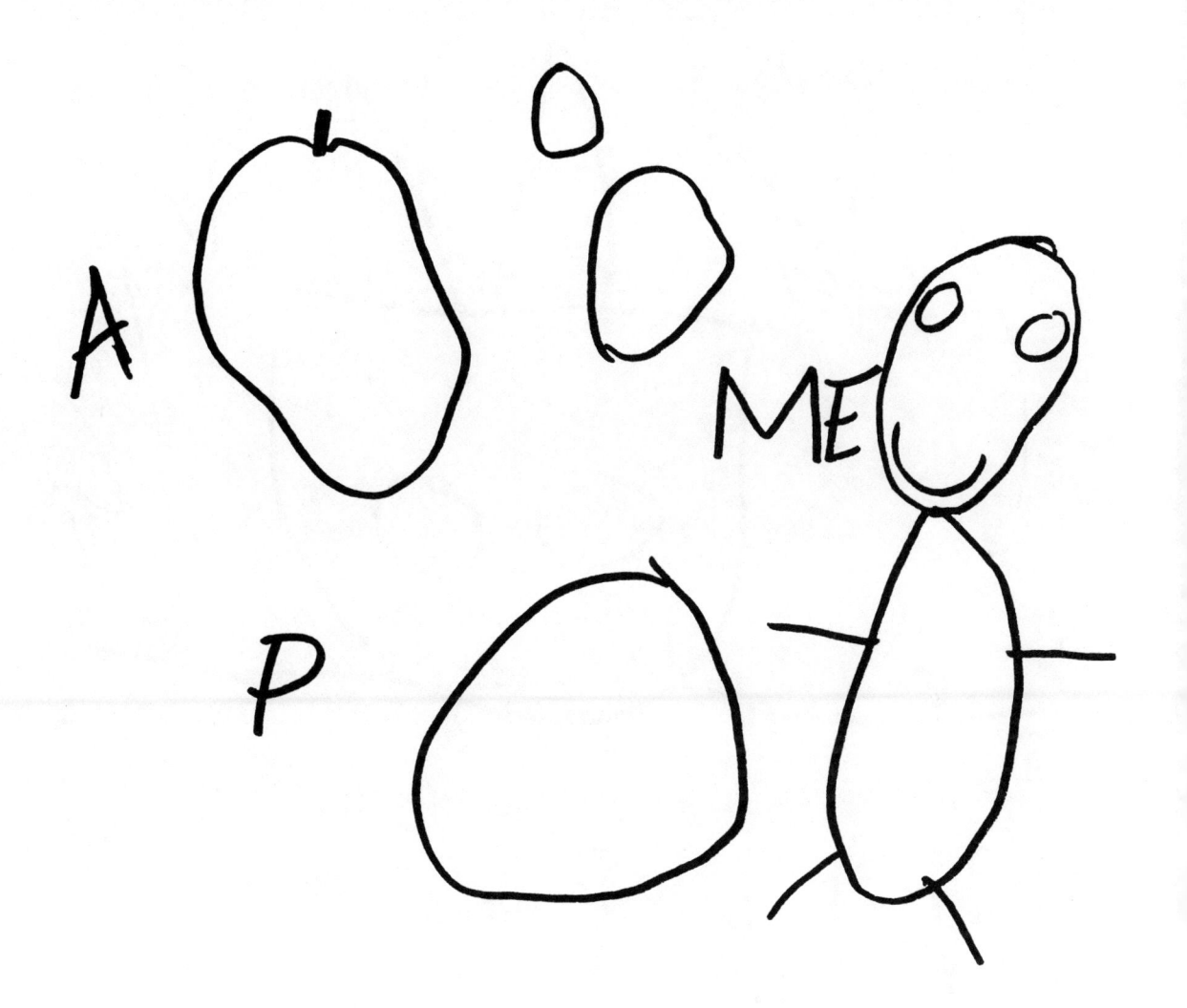

45

Jan's Work *Figure 2–1*

Teachers Telling Their Stories

Figure 2–2   *Danny's Work*

LF.LKT

Trevor spends a great deal of time on his intricate dinosaur drawing (Figure 2–3), while talking to the other children about the characteristics of different dinosaurs. He is particularly impressed by the gigantic size of many dinosaurs. When I ask him to write he says, "Oh, you mean like a book," and proceeds to write: "One time long, long ago brachiosaurus weighed as heavy as ten elephants." Trevor's concern with correct spelling causes him to put periods after brachiosaurus and elephants because "Those are long words. I can't spell them. So I made them abbreviations." Trevor works independently. He is eager to share his knowledge but does not require continuous support from me.

Two groups of children will write today. In three days' time, all the children will have written in the small group at the table. They will write about fire engines, racing cars, rainbows, houses, their families, their pets. All of them will be successful. Johnson, with his limited knowledge of English, turns out to know the alphabet. A fine artist, he carefully executes his picture, and when I point to the rabbit in his drawing and say, "rabbit," he follows the model of the other children and writes "RB" at the top of his paper.

Some of the children's topics may be the same, for the ideas of one child will stimulate similar ideas in another. But as the children realize that they have many stories that will interest their classmates, and as they come to understand that they choose their own topics for writing, they write their own ideas in their own voices. No two children write alike. The process, topics, and language of every child emerge as distinct as those of Jan, Danny, and Trevor on this first morning.

After the children finish this initial writing, each chooses a "journal" and learns where to store it in the class file. We discuss what to do with the first pieces of writing and decide to put them on the bulletin board. We block off a section for each child and put the writing there.

During the second week of school, the children begin drawing and writing in their journals in a total group environment. They do only one page a day for the first few weeks of school as I encourage them to take their time and explore their ideas in the pictures and script that combine to form their writing. My responses to their efforts focus on the content of their pieces of writing, ignore errors in mechanics, and encourage them to revise by adding more information. These conferences are short, and in the beginning of the year, I attempt to see each child every day. The writing time each day begins with a mini-lesson, a term Lucy Calkins (1986) uses to describe this brief, focused teaching strategy. My mini-lessons for writing workshop are based on observations I make of one or more children during the writing time. Generally, these lessons fall into one of four categories described by Mary Ellen Giacobbe (1987): (1) pro-

48   Teachers Telling Their Stories

Figure 2–3   Trevor's Work

ONE TIME LOG LOG AGO BCEOSU. WEAID AS HIVE AS TEN ELAFN.

cedures for the writing workshop, such as workshop rules or the organization and location of writing materials; (2) skill areas, such as punctuation or spelling strategies; (3) strategies for writing, such as topic selection or adding information; and (4) qualities of good writing, such as effective leads and endings or writing to "show" rather than "tell." We conclude each writing workshop with a large group sharing time. We gather in a circle on the rug and one or two children read their writing and receive responses from the entire group.

As the year progresses, the children write longer pieces. They learn to select and staple paper and to keep writing folders for their work. They incorporate revision and editing skills and *publish* pieces in books that become part of the classroom library. Some writings will emerge from the curriculum and from situations within the total school setting. For example, Oliver and Justin write a letter to the teacher who supervises school safety patrols to complain about conditions for crossing the street. Several children write to and receive responses from authors whose books they enjoy. Note writing becomes an important means of communicating within the classroom. Writing becomes a natural part of the learning process in content areas of the curriculum (Avery 1987).

Reading Workshop

Before we go to lunch on this first day of school, I ask the children to choose two books from those in the room and place them on their desks. When we come back from lunch I conduct my first mini-lesson for reading workshop.

"People read in lots of ways," I tell the class. "I'm going to show you some of the ways they read." I again pick up *The Three Billy Goats Gruff*. "Sometimes people read aloud like we did this morning when we read this book. They read all the words and use lots of expression. Sometimes they read silently like this, saying the words in their heads to themselves." I demonstrate reading silently. "Sometimes people read by looking at the pictures and telling the story by what they see happening in the pictures." I begin to go through *The Three Billy Goats Gruff*, talking about each picture, describing what I see in detail, constructing a story, and forming questions about possible developments. "Often when people finish a book, they go back and look through it again. Sometimes they read the book again. Good readers think about what they've read—what it was about, what it means to them, why they like it or don't like it."

The mini-lesson has taken only a few minutes. I explain to the children that this is our reading workshop and now they will read the books they have chosen just as I have shown them with *The Three Billy Goats Gruff*. As they eagerly open their books I begin to circulate among them.

I stoop down to Julie's desk and notice that she is pointing to the book title and making the sound of the first letter, *s*. "What is your book about?" I ask.

"I don't know," she replies shyly. She points to a small black fish. "I didn't open it yet, but I think it's about a fish because there's this black fish on the cover. Only, I know *fish* begins with *f* and this word starts with *s*."

"I think you're right. Julie, the title of this book is the name of that fish." Julie moves her finger under the word *Swimmy*. "I bet you know the sounds *s* and *w* make."

Together, Julie and I make the consonant sounds and blend them together. "Swim?" Julie suddenly says.

"Pretty close! It's Swimmy!" Julie smiles, opens the book, and I move across the room to Matthew's desk.

"Tell me about your book?" I ask. The book is closed and Matthew is gazing around the room. Matthew looks at me for a moment. "I don't know," he says. I find the first page and ask Matthew what he sees. "A bear."

"Could the book be about that bear?"

"Yeah," he replies as he looks at me and smiles. I suggest to Matthew that he look at the book's pictures to see what happens to the bear. As he turns to the book I move on.

Sarah is chanting softly to herself as I stoop down by her desk. "I've got a Mother Goose book," she says. "I know some of these." She is looking at the pictures and repeating the familiar rhymes.

"Let's do it again," I say when she finishes. As she begins, I chant with her and follow the words in the text with my finger as we move through the stanza. "Can you do that?" I ask after the last line.

"Uh-huh." Sarah smiles as I leave and then puts her finger on the next line to continue on her own.

When I come to Laura she tells me, "I know this word and this word and these words, but I don't know this word in the middle. 'Oh, a ... we will go.'"

"This book's a song! Maybe you've heard it. Let's read together." I point to the words as we read "Oh, a ..." I make the sound of the letter *h*, pause, and continue, "we will go." Laura's eyes go to the picture on the page, back to the text, and then she reads "'Oh, a *hunting* we will go!' I got it now." She goes back to the book. I move on.

The reading workshop continues this way for ten or fifteen minutes. When I sense the children becoming restless, I know it is time to end for now. To conclude the session, I ask several children to tell the group about their books. Michael volunteers that he found a book about dinosaurs and he shows the group the picture of tyrannosaurus rex. Julie tells about the fish named Swimmy. She adds that the book says "Swimmy" on the front and she found a place inside the book that says "Swimmy" too.

"I read the *Hungry Caterpillar* book," says Dustin, holding it high in the air. I am pleased that Dustin announces that he has *read* the book. When I stopped at his desk he was retelling the story, his voice rising and falling with inflection, although not reading with word-by-word accuracy. What is important at this time is that Dustin sees himself as a reader and strives to form meaning from the text using a variety of resources—recall of the read-aloud, illustrations, his own sense of story, as well as clues from initial consonants. Another day Dustin will share his *reading* of the text with the entire class during our literature period. We will talk about his strategies, and his demonstration will provide a model for all the children.

In the next few days my mini-lessons will introduce particular books and deal with book selection, initial consonants, picture clues, left-to-right progression, and procedures for establishing our reading workshop. As the year goes on, I will present skills and strategies for reading, always focusing on forming meaning from the text. As with the mini-lessons for writing workshop, I will base the focus of these lessons on my observations of one or more children in the class as well as on reflections on my own personal reading experiences. I will encourage the children to use those strategies that are most efficient and effective for them and that develop from their natural learning style. As they become proficient, I will nudge them to use other strategies in order to become strong readers. The daily reading workshop will provide an opporunity for children to use and refine their reading skills as they engage in actual reading.

Understanding Differences

When I began examining learning in my classroom, I discovered a rich diversity of approaches to learning among the children in the class. No two children learn alike. As the year progresses, all develop and mature as learners and, in that maturing process, move toward a general conformity in understanding and concept development. Yet they all retain and develop their distinct individual styles and personalities, of which learning is one function.

When Donald Graves (1978–81b) began his research on the writing processes of young children, he expected to identify developmental stages. However, in the final report of his study he wrote:

> *Many similarities were seen among the children when they wrote, but as the study progressed, individual exceptions to the data increased in dominance. In short every child had behavioral characteristics that applied to that child alone. It is our contention that such variability demands a waiting responsive type of teaching. (29)*

After several years of observing young learners in my first-grade classroom, I have not seen any two children with identical writing *or* reading styles and processes. I have found that a "waiting responsive type of teaching"—a learner-centered approach—not only reveals the idiosyncratic processes of young learners, but it also enables writing and reading skills to develop and individuals to flourish. I cannot teach writing effectively without an individualized and responsive teaching style. This realization has led me to adopt a responsive approach to learners in all areas of the curriculum.

Talking—the dialogue between teacher and learner and among learners—becomes an important aspect of this waiting, responsive approach. Talking allows learners to explore their ideas and their options as they engage in learning. As learners make choices they develop confidence, thinking skills, and responsibility. I found that by waiting and listening before responding to children I gained a better understanding of the needs of a particular child. My assumptions about what learners needed changed and I began responding to individuals. I now see each child as my informant, an authority on his or her own learning process.

Harste, Burke, and Woodward (1984) report their work with the literacy development of young children in *Language Stories and Literacy Lessons*. Their research challenges traditional understanding of language learning.

> *...the most prevalent view of language development can be represented by a formula which states that: AGE in relationship to CONVENTION indicates GROWTH.*
>
> *In contrast to this view of development, we would suggest a new formula in which EXPERIENCE is seen as TRANSACTING with PRINT SETTINGS, the re-*

sults of which lead to new levels of PSYCHOLINGUISTIC AND SOCIOLINGUISTIC ACTIVITY. Because this process is cyclic and ongoing throughout life, the nature of literacy iteself is forever changing, creating new personal and societal potentials for all of us. (30)

The scope and sequence chart in basal reading programs typifies "the prevalent view" about language growth that Harste mentions. Educators tend to believe that children must learn language skills in a prescribed sequence and at specific ages and grade levels. For instance, the use of quotation marks or paragraphing in writing might be considered a "third-grade skill" and would be presented to the learner only after other specific skills were mastered. Harste renounces this idea and indicates that the encounters that learners have with language in natural and meaningful situations create an ongoing and evolving development in language growth that continues throughout life.

When addressing the implications of their findings Harste et al. write:

The focus of language in use is meaning. Instructional activities should not isolate the systems of language for formal study, but rather, should be natural and functional parts of the child's exploration of reading and writing as they use written language to explore their world....Which features of written language are learned and in what order they are learned is a function of context, purpose, interest, and the background of experience of the language learner. (205–6)

In the environment of my classroom, children may now pursue learning by reading books of their own choosing and writing stories based on their own experiences and backgrounds. Such involvement with written language, coupled with interactions within the classroom community, allows children to engage in a variety of meaning-making experiences that foster language learning. The talk in the classroom between the children and me and among the children themselves contributes to the children's language development. Our dialogue serves as a way to form ideas, to analyze and clarify thinking, and to teach and learn from each other. We use spoken language in natural ways in the school setting as we strive to form meaning together. Our different approaches and ideas enrich our understanding. We are a learning community.

When I encouraged other than traditional ways of learning in my classroom, I discovered that students were able to capitalize on their

The ultimate importance of language and literacy lies in the functions they perform and the uses they serve in an individual's life.

strengths while they developed weaker areas. A child-centered approach to teaching enables children to learn in individually efficient ways because it acknowledges differences among learners.

In his work with "multiple intelligences," Howard Gardner (1986) suggests that schools deal primarily with two ways of knowing: mathematical and verbal. But there are other ways of understanding, of learning, says Gardner. As he states:

> *The single most important contribution education can make to a child's development is to help him toward a field where his talents best suit him, where he will be satisfied and competent.... We should spend less time ranking children and more time helping them to identify their natural competencies and gifts, and cultivate those. There are hundreds and hundreds of ways to succeed, and many, many different abilities that will help you get there. (23)*

Differences in students are not limited to learning styles. Classrooms are no longer socially or culturally homogenous. This first-grade group is an example. Twenty-four children make up this class; the age span between the youngest and the oldest is twenty-two months. Of the twenty-four, ten are from families touched by divorce. Seven now live in single-parent homes, and three are supported by welfare. One child is a Chinese-American whose parents do not speak English and who maintain the Chinese language and culture in their home. Another culture is represented by a child who is a native of Trinidad. One child was hospitalized recently as a result of a parental beating. Another lives with an abusive, alcoholic father. Ten children in the class began kindergarten a year earlier in a different geographical community. Only six children in this first-grade class reside in two-parent families that reflect traditional American culture, in which one parent is the breadwinner and the primary task of the other is nurturing the family. Before another year passes, two more will move out of this category. Ten or fifteen years ago this diverse composite of children was unusual. Today this is not so.

Shirley Brice Heath states that diversification is not a trend in American culture, it is reality. The metaphor for American society, says Heath, is no longer a melting pot but rather, a *mosaic*. As part of this rich, vibrant mosaic, the children in American classrooms now come from a variety of backgrounds and cultures; in addition, many carry emotional burdens. All of these are factors that influence their learning processes. Heath points out that recognizing and responding to diversity among learners is an issue American education will need to confront.

...cultural diversity was not addressed as a problem to be dealt with but as a resource to be cultivated.

In the environment of a child-centered classroom, children learn to value each other despite differences and, at the same time, learn through collaboration rather than competition. Central to education is the use of language. A child-centered classroom encourages learners to use language to understand their world and each other and as a tool for learning.

Glenda Bissex (1980) states that "the logic by which we teach is not always the logic by which children learn" (199). When I taught in a traditional mode through a variety of prescribed program materials, I often felt that my teaching did not correlate with the children's potential as learners. I have learned that by responding to individuals rather than to group norms, and by encouraging meaning-making through the natural use of language in the classroom, I am able to honor diversity among young learners. I find that such an approach unmasks hidden potential and talent in children who do not learn by traditional methods or come from traditional home settings. I now strive to understand and respect the ways in which children are different as well as the ways in which they are alike, and to make the logic by which I teach akin to the logic by which children learn, so that *all* of the children become active participants in our literate community.

REFERENCES

Asbjornsen, Peter C., and Jorgen Moe. 1957. *The Three Billy Goats Gruff.* Il. Marcia Brown. New York: Harcourt.

Atwell, Nancie. 1985. "Writing and Reading from the Inside Out." In *Breaking Ground: Teachers Relate Reading and Writing in the Elementary School*, ed. Jane Hansen et al. Portsmouth, N.H.: Heinemann.

Avery, Carol S. 1987. "First Grade Thinkers Becoming Literate." *Language Arts* 64:611–18.

Bissex, Glenda. 1980. *GNYS AT WRK: A Child Learns to Write and Read.* Cambridge, Mass.: Harvard University Press.

Calkins, Lucy McCormick. 1986. *The Art of Teaching Writing.* Portsmouth, N.H.: Heinemann.

Carle, Eric. 1969. *The Very Hungry Caterpillar.* New York: Philomel.

Emig, Janet. 1987. Presentation at the Conference of the Coalition of English Associations, Queenstown, Md. July 15.

Gardner, Howard. 1986. "Rethinking the Value of Intelligence Tests." *New York Times*, 9 Nov. 1986, Education Life Section: 23–27.

Giacobbe, Mary Ellen. 1987. Presentation to the Manheim Township School District. Lancaster, Penn. August.

Graves, Donald H., for the Committee on Research, National Council of Teachers of English. 1978–81a. Articles initiated at the Writing Process Laboratory, University of New Hampshire, Durham, N.H., and published in the "Research Update" section of *Language Arts*.

Graves, Donald H. 1978–81b. *Final Report: A Case Study Observing the Development of Primary Children's Composing, Spelling, and Motor Behaviors During the Writing Process*, with collected papers and articles initiated at the Writing Process Laboratory. Durham, N.H.: University of New Hampshire.

———. 1983. *Writing: Teachers and Children at Work*. Portsmouth, N.H.: Heinemann.

Harste, Jerome C., Virginia A. Woodward, and Carolyn L. Burke. 1984. *Language Stories and Literacy Lessons*. Portsmouth, N.H.: Heinemann.

Heath, Shirley Brice. 1987. Address at the Conference of the Coalition of English Associations, Queenstown, Md. July 13.

Lionni, Leo. 1963. *Swimmy*. New York: Pantheon.

Rice, Inez. 1957. *The March Wind*. New York: Lothrop, Lee and Shepard.

White, E. B. 1952. *Charlotte's Web*. New York: Harper.

3

Kids and Computers
Who's on First?
C. JANE HYDRICK

It was November. I looked around the second-grade classroom and wondered, "When did I lose control? Did I give it up? Did I ever have it?" There were signs of control but all activity went on independent of me. The children were all involved in research tasks but needed me only occasionally:

"How do you spell 'turquoise'?"
"How do we call up the spelling checker?"
"Does this look like a buffalo? Tiffany says it looks like a bear."
"Can you laminate these for us?"

The room was buzzing with second graders by themselves or in small groups, reading, writing, drawing, cutting and pasting, discussing, arguing—in the midst of a myriad of projects both ongoing and completed. All the projects and materials in the room centered on one subject: Native

Americans. Resource books and picture collections were sorted by tribe or subject and piled on desk tops. The walls were covered with murals depicting several aspects of tribal life, and three-dimensional Native American art projects covered one long table in the back of the room. Clay pots, fashioned from play dough and modeling clay and illustrating the differences among Hopi, Navajo, Pueblo, and Apache designs, were grouped together with hastily written scratch-paper labels. Next to them were models of the Iroquois longhouses, Plains teepees, and Southwest hogans molded by young hands from playground mud and sticks and ready to be placed on a multicolored floor map of the United States. Six computers were being used, some with word processing, some with a data base on Native American tribes that the whole class had designed and created.

One group of four second graders was sprawled on the floor, source books, printouts of data base sorts, early word processing drafts, and assorted bits of paper littered about them. One group member, sporting a paper bag vest and feathered headband, sat at a computer terminal, awaiting directions from the others in her group. They were gathering more information on Seminoles to add to the Seminole tribe portion of the data base.

"Wait, Autumn, stay there [at the terminal] 'cause we need more stuff on Seminoles."

"Like what?"

"I don't know."

"How 'bout the alligators?"

"We already have 'em on 'special' [a field in the data base]. Besides, they weren't really Seminoles."

"But they helped 'em."

"What about Sequoyah?"

"He was a Cherokee. See? He's already in the data base."

"Well, what about the Seminole chief? They had one too."

"Yeah—let's add him. Osceola. He was cool."

"How do you spell his name?"

"Mmm. Angela, you look it up."

"Where do we add him?"

"Here—it has to go in 'special.' That's where he fits."

Much of what this particular study group had gathered on Seminoles had already been added.

Data bases were nothing new to these second graders. On the second day of their second-grade school year, these children had created a data base of the class members. The data base, appropriately entitled "The

Kids and Computers

World's Greatest Second Grade," had as its fields first name, last name, address, city, state, telephone number, birthday, pets, number of kids in the family, favorite food, favorite drink, favorite color, favorite movie, favorite cartoon, favorite toy, favorite activity, and favorite book. There were a number of issues to be resolved, or at least tentatively agreed upon, for the sake of consistency in wording so that computer sorts would be truly reflective of the information in the data base.

"April, pepperoni pizza is really pizza. Come on."
"But I don't like other kinds, just pepperoni."
"Look, Autumn's favorite is pepperoni too. Besides, if you change then we'll have fourteen people who love pizza."
"Okay, but I only like pepperoni, that's all."

Issues such as classifying G.I. Joe as a doll and referring to an activity as "skateboarding" rather than "riding a skateboard" were not resolved with equal dispatch!

"G.I. Joe is not a doll! Only girls play with dolls. They're sissy."
"Ha! Dolls are little fake people and G.I. Joe is a little fake people."
"But he's different. You don't dress him up in dresses and stuff and take him out on dates and stupid stuff."
"Alex! You dress up your G.I. Joe."
"Yeah, but not in dresses and stupid stuff, in real Army gear."
"Real? Oh, I'm so sure. Give me a break, Alex."
"Well, not real, but [it] looks like real. Anyway, it isn't stupid."

At times, I took the liberty of stepping into a discussion in an effort to turn it from an emotional issue (determining the degree of reality of G.I. Joe and other dolls) to one of definition (Could G.I. Joe and Barbie both be included in a field entitled "LFP," little fake people?). In this case, the boys eventually agreed to including G.I. Joe in LFP even though G.I. Joe's Army gear was, in their eyes, considerably less fake than Barbie's elaborate and "stupid" outfits. Ironically, the boys who had Cabbage Patch Kids of their own did not consider them dolls at all because they didn't really play with them. They regarded the Cabbage Patch Kids as "their friends and just changed their clothes once in a while." The girls agreed. Cabbage Patch Kids were their kids, not their toys. Thus, Cabbage Patch Kids remained out of the debate entirely.

Each child entered his or her personal information in the data base. After all the children had entered their information, the class embarked on sorting. They sorted by street name, by favorite drink (the Coca-Cola/Pepsi debate was overshadowed by chocolate milk shakes), by favorite food (fourteen children chose pizza), by favorite movie (*Rambo* was outnumbered by *Never-Ending Story*) and so on. With a little guidance from me, they progressed to computer sorts that combined fields (all children born in January who like pizza and skateboarding or all children born in the summer who like skiing and chocolate). With a little further guidance from me, they applied their various sorts to questions, word problems and bar graphs (How many more pizza-loving skateboarders are there than fudge-adoring bicyclers? Is the bar in the graph longer for *Rambo* or for *Never-Ending Story* and what does that mean?). Their enthusiasm over sorting led them to expand their audience. They developed questions and word problems around the sorting printouts, which they took home for siblings, parents, and grandparents to answer.

The children were so comfortable with developing fields of information, with sorting, and with printing out that when the study of Native Americans began, soon after Halloween was packed away, the children thought of a data base as a natural medium for sorting the information they had begun to collect on various tribes.

In the beginning of the study, the fields reflected the information the children had gathered on the first Native American tribe, such as crops planted and kachina names. As their study progressed, and as fields became inappropriate and more information was added to fields already strained to their limits, the children changed and added fields, filling in gaps on tribes they had already studied and entered in the data base. The study of the first tribe had yielded a body of facts, but during the study of the second tribe, knowing that they were creating a data base, the children began formulating generalizations that could be confirmed by their knowledge of both tribes. These preliminary generalizations became the field for the data base: home type, land type, and so on. The final data base fields they agreed on were tribe name, location, land type, home type, nomad (y/n), farmer (y/n), war/peace, power (men or women), and several fields labeled "special" in which information peculiar to that tribe was entered.

To obtain information on tribes, the children took advantage of a variety of sources: filmstrips and films, nonfiction books, picture- and chart-rich books for the nonreaders (who by this time had learned how to "read" pictures for information and generalizations), telephone calls to museums, and interviews with local pioneers and tribal officers. Because the children had grown in their awareness of biased perspectives, they even included in their research some Hollywood cowboy and Indian spectaculars—examples of blatant bias, which the chidlren were now able to view at least somewhat askance. The children included in their awareness of multiple perspectives the biases of people writing nonfiction books, the biases of historians, and, on a more personal and introspective note, the additional biases of the readers and interpreters of nonfiction.

The children continued to refer to their sources, making additional notes and adding more to the data base. The information in the data base grew and the children compared and contrasted tribes based on the information in the fields they had created. Much information was left out because of the constraints of field number and size. However, the children viewed this as just another function of biased perspective and were less concerned, at least for the moment, with the fact that the information was selected and limited than they were with the actual selection of information to include.

"Why do we have to put jerky *and* pemmican under Sioux? Why not just jerky?"
"Because they're different."
"But not really. They're both food and they're dried."
"But who ever eats pemmican?"
"That's right. So we gotta know about it."
"Yuk. I hate jerky."
"You'd love it if you'd die 'cause there wasn't nothin' else!"
"Yuk. I still hate it. Okay, we'll put it in. But I still hate it."

For these second graders, a study of Native American tribes did not involve memorizing names, dates, places, or pot designs. Assorted bits of paper and later the computer, not their memories, would store all those facts. Rather, what the children learned was that they themselves controlled both the quantity and quality of facts and that their ultimate task was not simply to record and transmit information but, through their own generation of hypotheses, to transform that body of information to create new meaning and new knowledge. The computer, through the data base application, was the children's tool. It would store and recall facts while they determined what facts would be included and the new shape those facts would take. There was no doubt in the children's minds who was in control: who was master, who was slave.

Since the second day of school in September, these second graders had come to take the six classroom computers for granted just as they took other tools for granted: pencils, paper, crayons, scissors. But for them the computers had become a different kind of tool, a tool that could do more than re-create the memorize-recite cycle to which they were already accustomed. The computers did the memorizing and reciting, while the children dictated what information would be memorized and how and why the information would be recited. The children were empowered by both machines and knowledge. They controlled their data base by selecting sources of information, and selecting from these the information to be included and a perspective for that information. They controlled the purpose of their information-gathering. They controlled the end product of their information-gathering. Thus they controlled both the content and the purpose of their learning. This was not the first time in their lives that the control had been theirs, but this time it seemed so much more obvious because there were now complicated machines responding to their commands, storing, handling, and sorting information to their specifications.

The sense of control that the children gained through the manipulation of the computers empowered them in many areas of the curriculum. In contrast, the first inkling I had of my own "loss of control" was during the first phase of the unit on Native Americans, which I had designed several years before. This first phase involved posting a "bearskin" on the wall with a picture story on it. The "bearskin" was brown butcher paper that had been soaked and crunched until it was soft and leatherlike and then cut into the shape of a large bearskin. The picture story was a short story, using sign symbols I had discovered in researching a Southwest tribe, that depicted a tribesman who leaves his teepee for three days to go on a camping trip. As in other years, the children delighted in decoding the pictures to tell the story in words. My plan then, as in other years, was to teach them other sign symbols they could then use to write stories of their own and then to have them trade stories with each other in peer groups to "read" and edit for content in order to arrive at a consensus translation. Around the bearskin story I had stapled thirty or forty other sign symbols. As I was telling the children the correct translation for each symbol, the children began telling me why each symbol was valid or not and, if a symbol was not valid in their eyes, what symbol might be substituted for it. What followed was a three-day project in which the children each came up with individual symbol systems that, after feedback from peer groups and individual friends, they could use to create symbol stories for others to "read" and enjoy. The liveliest discussions were those that centered on the differences in symbols for "mother," "woman," and "teacher" and for intangibles or qualities such as "beautiful" or "love." Even actions such as "hit" or "shoot" were subjects for debate. The easiest to illustrate were objects such as "tree" and "house," although the children became very involved in a clarification of tree: desert tree, pine tree, broadleaf tree, tree in summer or tree in winter. And the symbolization of "house" brought into the discussion aspects such as the effect of climate on roof slant or building material or basic house shape. The children knew that flat roofs were typical of homes in the southwest and peaked roofs of homes in the northern states, but had not reasoned why until the discussion of symbols for "house." Once they accepted the fact that snow piling up on a flat roof could collapse it, they turned to the pictures of teepees. Surely these homes were not slanted because of snow dangers. And what of igloos, which existed in snow country but which were not slanted? The whole question of generalization and rule-making became a fascinating one to them.

Eventually, not only the stories but the symbols themselves were the children's. Since no misspellings or mechanical errors were possible, all editing focused on content and on each author's ability to transmit a concept through a symbol. Symbol stories popped up on bear-shaped construction paper, butcher paper "bearskin," journal sheets, and any readily available writing space. The stories were penciled, inked, crayoned, and painted. One morning on the way into the classroom, I stepped over a symbol story that had been written stealthily during the night with colored chalk. An editing group pounced on it before the first bell rang and the class was treated to a revised version during recess. Storywriting and sharing and rewriting were more popular than recess for several weeks. As an exciting extension of their audience, the children took their symbol stories to family members, friends in other classes, and even to nonreaders in the kindergarten classes. What a thrill to have someone not "into" the study of Native Americans as we were be able to read and interpret a symbol story! The symbols were neither mine nor those of any Native American tribe; they were the children's. The children took sole responsibility for their creation and sole responsibility for their ability to transmit meaning in stories. What empowerment they derived from the success of their undertaking! Now they were able to command all facets of their language.

Meanwhile, the data base swelled with information from the children's research. Some of the activities that evolved from the work with the data base did so because of the children's need for additional media for the information they were gathering—media that were separate and different from the data base. For example, when they were filling in the particulars for each tribe under the "special" fields, they quickly ran out of room for more than key words. The children soon became impatient with this and looked for some other medium to express what they had come to know about the various tribes. I suggested word processing as a possible solution. They had already become familiar with word processing during September and October and agreed that they could enter notes as text on their own or as a group and then write sentences around the notes at a later time. Melissa, Sara, and Autumn wrote this piece on Seminoles around a list of notes they had collected during their research:

...the concern of English instruction in the elementary school is to help individual children develop into confident and capable language users.

The Seminole Indians were peaceful and they didn't move around alot. They lived in houses with no sides and stilts held the houses up. They had alot of game like fish and they were alligators in the swamps. The men built dome shaped wigwams. Out of clam shells they made beads and made dresses and necklaces with them. They put the fish around the fire and that makes them dry out so they can keep them longer. The white men tried to steal their land but the white men got lost in the swamps. It was so dark in the swamps that they couldn't see. The Seminoles never had to surrendered. They let the alligators do all the work. They always had trees in the swamps and it was warm in the swamps and it was nice weather. They were a great tribe. They never had to fight because they were peaceful people. They made their own canoes to go through the swamps.

By this time, the children had drifted into many small groups, members overlapping, to research particular items or subjects of interest. Melissa, Sara, and Autumn chose to write about the Seminoles, but they also worked with Damon and Kempe, who were fascinated with weapons and did a comparative study of weapons across the tribes. Angela, Robert, and Heather began with a study on art and narrowed it down to a delightful collection of masks. All this specialization posed a dilemma: not everyone in the class would be familiar with information on all the tribes. Was it important that they all be? Surely not for the sake of any assessment I might impose on them. They admitted that they wanted to share what they had learned with each other and agreed that word processing would be a medium through which they would have text to share. As a result, they planned a class book and delegated chapters to those who had researched particular areas of interest. The chapters consisted of word processing text, drawings, and charts. All final copies were mounted on construction paper and bound between two large bearskin-covered boards.

Convinced that their material should have a wide reader audience and that their data base was a concise summary of much of the information included in the chapter texts, the children wanted to investigate other media as well—in particular, media that would utilize the data base. They decided on two: a set of questions drawn from information in the data base and a crossword puzzle drawn from information listed in the data base but elaborated upon in the chapter texts.

The set of questions progessed from straightforward ones, such as "Where did the Zuni live?" to those that required more comparative anal-

Testing has become the enemy of a learner-centered curriculum...

ysis, such as "What was the same about the Zuni, the Pueblo, the Navajo, the Apache, and the Hopi?" And "How many tribes lived in home types that could not be moved?"

The creation of a crossword puzzle posed a new problem. It required the puzzle creators to understand the essence of questions and clues. The art of giving a clue without giving the answer is a fine art and one, as I realized not too far into the activity, not easily refined in second grade. The children finally came up with a list of answers and then wrote short clues that, as they had determined, could not mention the answer. Two days later, they had the clues and word list ready to enter into *Crossword Magic*, a computer program from Mindscape that creates the crossword form from user-entered clues and words.

The children were excited about the question set and the crossword puzzle. Determined to share them with as many others as possible, they devised a contest. The data base, set of questions, and crossword puzzle were duplicated as a package with a cover letter explaining that the B4 second graders were conducting a contest. The first person—or class—to submit the correct answers for either the question set or the crossword puzzle would win a prize. With all the second graders sworn to secrecy so that the answer key would not be leaked, the contest packets were distributed on Monday. By Wednesday, the children had two tie winners, publicity, limelight, and the respect of every student and adult in the attendance area.

A striking contrast to this scene involving confident, computer-literate language users was one I confronted in the evenings when I taught computer awareness to adults at the Computer Institute. What a difference there was between the adults and the second graders just in their attitude toward control over the computer. The adults approached the computer as if it were a dreadful, controlling machine that must, through practice and effort, in turn be controlled so that they could do their jobs. The second graders were also concerned with control, but they approached the question of control with eagerness and an enthusiasm for gaining more and more mastery of the machine for their own purposes. For the second graders, each character key, each function was not an obstacle to mastery, as it was with the adults, but was instead another step toward ultimate mastery of the machine and another tool in an electronic tool kit they would eventually use for their own purposes.

Word processing for these second graders was not simply another writing implement like colored ink pens or pickle-shaped pencils. Aside from the obvious advantages of perfectly formed characters, word processing provided the children with a medium in which they could experiment with spacing, with form, with the placement and sequence of text, with new characters, and with untraditional procedures and products. Word processing extended their realm of control and possibility.

That the children used their data bases for classifying and sorting illustrates their concept development. But the most exciting, involving learning appeared to come about when they studied the information they had plugged into their data bases and began to see links between facts, to analyze, to synthesize, and to make new knowledge from old facts.

"Sonny, look at all the tribes that were warlike. They're all on this side of the page [on the printout]. These ones here [on this side of this page] didn't fight."

"Ooooh, neat. Eight of 'em did war and four of 'em did peace. I guess maybe they killed off the ones that did peace so there wasn't so many of 'em left. More war ones."

"Justin! You guys are so dumb! It doesn't matter where you put them on the paper if they did war or not."

"So what matters, Brooke?"

"Yeah! Here's the war, here's the peace. Right there. So what makes 'em one or the other, Brooke?"

Throughout the entire unit on Native Americans, the children had been responsible for questioning, gathering of sources, and noting information. They had created the fields for the data base, entered the information, and were now studying the printouts of their varied sorts. There was no doubt that they were skilled in gathering and manipulating information. Learning had become more than the memorize-recite cycle. Each area of the curriculum had become an exercise in problem solving. Siegler (1983) analyzed the role of knowledge in learning and defended its importance by stating that

> much of children's knowledge can be characterized as rules for solving problems. Essentially identical to the hypotheses formed by scientists, these rules are predictions that, under specific circumstances, particular outcomes will occur or particular actions will be taken. (631)

Thus, the knowledge that children already have about scientific and mathematical concepts does influence the way in which they acquire additional information. According to Siegler's research on problem solving,

...we hope that our concern for content as well as for process comes through.

experiences that disconfirm the rules children use seem to be crucial to the learning of new rules. However, such experiences alone often are insufficient; children may find themselves in the position of knowing that their rules are incorrect, but of not being able to formulate useful alternatives. (636)

In analyzing the information in the Native American data base, the second graders noted that warring tribes lived in mobile housing and peaceful tribes lived in permanent structures.

"Look, guys. See these tribes? They lived in teepees and they fought. The Hopi and the Navajo and these ones lived in these things [stationary hogans] and they were peaceful."

"I know why. 'Cause they could pack up real fast and get out o'there before the others could fight back."

"Yeah. And they didn't lose much either."

"They didn't have houses and furniture and slow animals and stuff to lose."

"And they didn't have to worry about growing food 'cause they hunted when they were moving."

The children were pleased with their hypothesis and excited that they had come up with a new idea. Then came the disconfirmation.

"Oh no! Wait! Look at the Nez Percé. And the Iroquois."

"Yeah. The Nez Percé lived in teepees but they were peaceful. And the Iroquois lived in those long houses and they were powerful and they fought."

"Maybe they just don't fit."

"But they have to!"

"No they don't."

"Well, let's make 'em fit."

And so they did attempt to "make 'em fit." They re-searched the source material and data base. They seemed primarily concerned with retaining their hypothesis and with finding data that would confirm their hypothesis. In support of their hypothesis, they concluded that there was error built into their data gathering: not only were their sources of information limited in number (school and home libraries), but the information they had selected from those sources was also limited by who had read and selected the information represented by the notes. They extended the built-in error to include the biases and limited information of the authors of the sources as well.

In the end, the children retained their hypothesis and concluded that the Nez Percé, though peaceful, lived in mobile housing because they had to provide pasture for the Appaloosa horses they bred. The Iroquois, they concluded, were so powerful that they could afford to live in permanent structures and not have to strike and flee. Besides, they added, it was the women of the Iroquois who had the power, and everyone knows that women want permanent structures! The Iroquois, too, had based their tribal structure on the adoption of conquered tribes, so the war strategy was not so much one of attack and pillage as it was one of taking over and incorporating.

Joseph Weizenbaum, in an interview with Holly Brady in *Classroom Computer Learning* (1985), contested the use of word processors and data bases as tools of logic and reasoning: "I think that children have a power to imagine that is almost magical when compared to the adult imagination, and there is something irrecoverable that a child loses when he or she becomes bound by logic" (27). It seemed, in this second-grade classroom, that the data base did not bind the children to a rigid system of logic. Rather, it provided them with a system for storing and sorting their information—a framework that freed them to experiment with looking at the data in a much broader context than simply as separate facts. The data base was the means, not the end. It became a tool of logic, yes, but a tool limited only by the children's imaginations and their willingness to create questions rather than to seek answers. Freed from the constraints of data storage and the limitations of memory, the children were able to exercise their power to imagine. Once the transmission of information was complete, the transformation of information could take place.

We can present four major arguments for the use of data bases in the classroom. First, the data base facilitates the shift of control from the environment to the individual. The children, learning environment permitting, control what data will be entered and how it will be organized. The children also control how the data will finally be analyzed and synthesized. Second, by creating a data base, the children become aware of their own problem-solving skills and their ability to generate hypotheses, to make sense of a mass of data, and to make new knowledge from the old. Third, creation of a data base is rarely an isolated activity. The gathering of data, the creation of fields, the analysis and synthesis of data, the generation and testing of hypotheses—all demand a dialectic with peers, with teachers, and with the computer. Finally, not only are the data included in a data base a symbolic form, but the fields into which the data are placed are themselves symbols of the abstract classifications.

The development of a data base illustrates Vygotsky's phases in concept formation. The data children collect from their information sources can be regarded as a syncretic heap, what Vygotsky (1962) referred to when he said that "a child tends to merge the most diverse elements into one unarticulated image on the strength of some chance impression" (60). The chance impression may be formed by data grouped initially because of physical location (notes taken from the same source or by the notetaker on the same piece of paper), or because of physical appearance (pictures together, long notes together, short notes, sentences, sentence fragments together). In the next phase, the data collected are grouped in complexes: data are linked not only by children's subjective impressions, but by bonds that actually exist between the data. In this phase it is important that the teacher/learning environment permit children to generate their own hypotheses. If hypotheses are prestated by the teacher, then children will be parroting rather than developing concepts. Through generating and testing their own hypotheses, children will attain a level of genuine concept formation.

Participants in the Coalition Conference agreed on the importance of celebrating diversity in children and of applauding educational practices that endeavor to realize the promise of each child through language and language learning. Sadly, though, the typical second-grade classroom is not one in which children's diversities are celebrated—or even recognized—nor are opportunities for individuality through language encouraged. Despite a national trend toward acquiring more computers and toward using the computer as a tool, few second-grade classrooms have ready access to computers, and few have challenged students to use the computer as a tool to advance their own purposes and learning.

In a relatively short time it became apparent that a remarkable singularity in perspective existed among the individuals in the elementary strand.

The second graders in my classroom viewed not only the medium of information storage and handling—the data base and word processor—but the actual information—the data on Native Americans—as tools for their own thinking and their own creation of personal knowledge. The value of their projects and activities lay not in the book they coauthored, in the information they amassed on Native Americans, or in the questions, data base, or crossword puzzle they created, but rather in each child's worth as a learner, as a controller of his or her own content and purpose of learning. Everything served these learners: computers, books, resources, teachers, their own skills in reading, writing, and drawing. And each learner emerged from the experience not only more knowledgeable about Native Americans but more aware of his or her individual autonomy as a learner. These second graders gained skill in problem solving while developing a positive attitude toward knowledge and learning, which was due at least in part to their collaborative tasks with application software in the classroom.

I look back now on the questions I asked myself as I looked around the classroom in November: "When did I lose control? Did I give it up? Did I ever have it?" I began the year as I had every other year in my teaching career, with a notion of control as a matter of external restraint rather than personal command. By having the children use data bases and word processing to help them organize, store, and present their findings, I provided the children with a means to take command of their own learning. In terms of restraint, then, I lost whatever control three years of public school had imposed on the children's learning. In terms of command, the children gained more and more control as they became more and more empowered learners. Their control was never mine to have. It was theirs to have, and my responsibility was to help them discover and develop.

Who was on first, kids or computers? A tricky question. Did stones and sticks exist as tools before man first lifted one to strike? Stone Age man picked up the tools of his age, was empowered by using them, and changed his life. Today's children can be empowered by picking up the tools of the Information Age. Knowledge is changing, information is changing, occupations are changing, job skills and demands are changing. The people best equipped to survive in the Information Age and all subsequent "Ages" will be the ones who have the skills to cope with change: they will expect change, welcome its challenges, be agents of change themselves.

REFERENCES

Brady, H. 1985. "Hang on to the Power to Imagine." *Classroom Computer Learning* 3 (December): 24–27.

Siegler, R. S. 1983. "How Knowledge Influences Learning." *American Scientist* 4: 631–38.

Vygotsky, L. S. 1962. *Thought and Language.* Cambridge, Mass.: MIT Press.

4

Thinking Throughout the Process
Self-Evaluation in Writing
SUSAN STIRES

Seven years ago, at the beginning of the first year of our school writing project, most of my intermediate-level learning disabled students considered themselves failures as writers. But as they focused on expressing meaning and communicating with others in their writing throughout the year, they began to experience success, and both their concept of themselves as writers and their confidence in their abilities changed as their understanding, knowledge, and skill increased. As Donald Graves (1985) has written, "Although writing process work helps all writers, it seems to be particularly successful with people who see themselves disenfranchised from literacy" (36).

My students learned to write and to evaluate their writing. For ongoing evaluation, or what Thomas Hilgers (1986b) calls "forming," they evaluated pieces of writing in process, particularly during revision or editing. They also evaluated their pieces as products, which Hilgers calls "summing up." For overall evaluation we looked at their collected writing every nine weeks and at the end of the year. They chose the pieces they liked best and least and talked about the reasons for their choices. At the end of that first year, I asked my students to write a self-evaluation in which they would tell how they changed or grew as writers from September to June. I also asked them to choose their best pieces for the year and tell why they selected as they did. They were to include the discoveries they had made about their own processes as writers. They had their folders to refer to and were allowed time to read and think about their writing. Except for the fact that this was an assigned topic for a specific audience—the student and me—this piece was to be written like other pieces during writing workshop; that is, it was to be developed over time, and each student was to draft, revise, confer, and edit. Shawn, a fourth grader, who had not considered himself a writer at the beginning of the year because of his spelling problems, wrote the reflective self-evaluation in Figure 4–1.

By contrast, the following text was written by a fourth grader on a recent state assessment.

> ... we must ... invest our efforts in developing [assessment] instruments and techniques that will help teachers to teach better in their classrooms.

Original Text	Conventional Form
At Harry Harry an I fun at he hous	At Harry's Harry and I [had] fun at his house.
A.T. is a nise kib an Harry to. we did sone brakbansing in a talint shoe we had alt of fun. I wish I was out side rite now. Sens I am not I will stoq thingcing a bowt it. I hope you relis I am not having fun good day. O I for got my frund's Ron and Jonhe Thay bo not hav mech more but I bo not care thay ar real nise and Heath he has a lrning bisa dlute so bo Rod. I hav bislexeal- u you bo not no hou hrd- This is fore me.	A.T. is a nice kid, and Harry [is] too. We did some breakdancing in a talent show. We had a lot of fun. I wish I was outside right now. Since I am not I will stop thinking about it. I hope you realize I am not having fun [a good day]. Oh, I forgot my friends, Ron and John. They do not have much more, but I do not care. They are real nice and Heath [is too]. He has a learning disability. So does Rod. I have dyslexia. You do not know how hard this is for me.

Thinking Throughout the Process

Shawn's Self-Evaluation

Figure 4–1

> Shawn
> This year I wrote 16 pieces. In third grade I didn't write any pieds. I have changed as the year went on. My pieces got longer and longer. Now I almost always put my punctuation.
> My best piece is when I wrote to the fire chief in Wiscasset. My reason for picking the fire chief piece is that I took my time writing it and I didn't make many mistakes I made it like a busines letter.
> I like to draft — just get it down with out correct spelling.
> My process is getting my feelings down, then revise, and I edit myself, and then have the techer edit it for me.

This state writing test is designed so that students can have the time and materials to draft, revise, and self-edit before writing their final copies into the test booklet. The students are given a writing prompt, in this case to write about a memory of having a good time with a friend or friends. Although this student attempted to stick to the topic, he was overwhelmed by the task and used writing to "talk" to the reader. Although he has strengths as a writer, he does not appear to know what they are or how to use them in this situation. His evaluation of himself is that he is dyslexic and is therefore excluded from this process. He is disenfranchised from literacy.

The primary students I now teach have labels like L.D., E.D., and E.M.R., but they are unaware of them. They value themselves as readers and writers because they know about their own reading and writing processes and because I value them as readers and writers. Obviously, I value them because they are inherently valuable, but I also overtly value them so that their other teachers will do likewise, and so that they will continue to value themselves. My kindergarten through third-grade students are considered to be the least sophisticated language users in the school, but in many ways they are no different from primary students in the regular program.

Writing and Responding

I provide time and opportunities for my students to make evaluative responses to questions, both formally in publishing conferences and interviews and informally as the occasions arise during conferences and other talks. I also share things about my own processes that help them evaluate theirs, and encourage them by laughing, or rolling my eyes, or running over to get a book in which a professional writer has done something similar to the student writer. My students' comments about their writing and reading have always been important to me. They know I value what they have to say, including their evaluations, because I listen to them, record what they say, and use the information they provide to plan activities, help them work with each other, and build their concepts of themselves as writers.

Of course, I am not the only teacher in the room. When I meet with my students in small groups, everyone is a teacher. Some of my students stay in their classrooms for writing, and I go to them, assisting their

Good teachers continuously reflect upon what they are doing in the classroom.... Their classrooms are research laboratories in which they instruct and modify instruction to make it better.

teachers. In this way, they receive responses from a large group—just as Danny did last year. His most consistent answer to why he chose to publish a particular book was, "The other kids will like it." Having an effect on a group in some way, attracting interest, revealing knowledge, or gaining approval, drives self-evaluation.

When I studied my students' self-evaluations, I learned that they occurred naturally at all stages of the writing process, from prewriting, to writing, to rewriting. In the next three sections, I will relate a few of the many situations in which students evaluated their writing. Most of the students featured are my primary resource room students; the rest are primary students in classrooms where I worked when my students were mainstreamed for writing. I have limited my examples to recorded teacher/student interactions, although another fertile area is student/student or group interactions.

Evaluating Beginnings: Drawing, Writing, Topics, and Modes

As a kindergartner, Kevin doesn't first select a topic and then begin to draw or talk about it. For him, drawing functions as the rehearsal for his writing and usually determines topic selection; in many ways, the drawing *is* the writing. If he were asked the question "What are you going to write about?" he would give the classic answer "I don't know. I haven't drawed it yet." When I talked to Kevin, he was already working on a second drawing, having rejected his first one (Figure 4–2). After we had talked about the one he was working on I asked him to tell me about the first one. He explained, "This is messed up." I asked what happened, and he continued, "The guy's head is too small inside the car. Donnie thought so, too. I'm writing on this one 'cause it's okay."

For Sarah, too, drawing and writing are closely combined in her evaluation of her piece (Figure 4–3). She had read her random string of letters as "The fisherman has crabs, fish, lobsters, and more crabs." When I asked her to tell me more about it, she simply said that it was nice. Thinking that she might be referring to the colors or to some other aspect of the drawing because she loves to draw, I asked, "What makes it nice?" She said, "It is about a fisherman, and I was at the Fisherman's Forum." Sarah's dad is a fisherman and her family had just attended this state

Figure 4–2 *Kevin's Drawing*

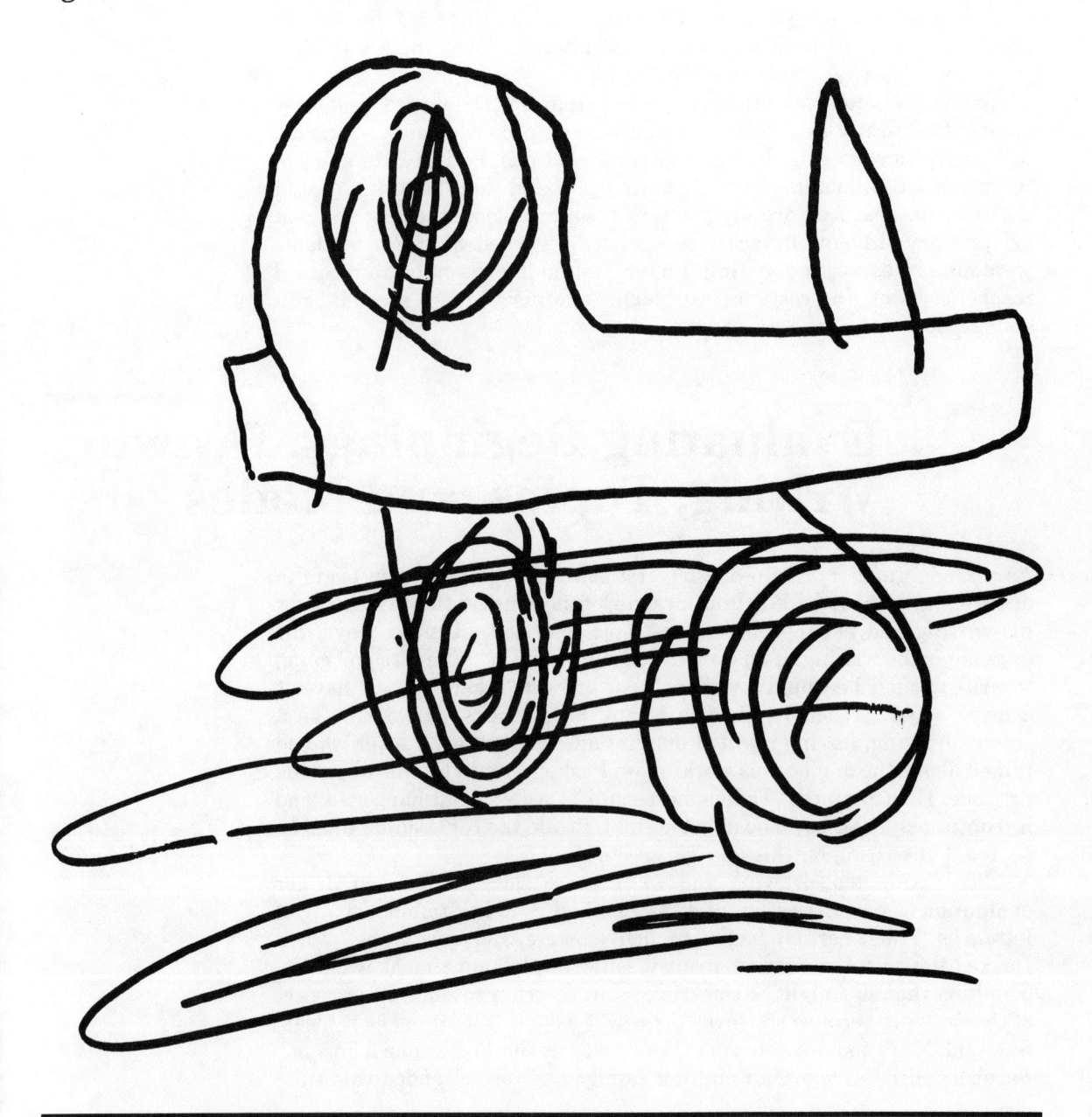

Thinking Throughout the Process

Sarah's Piece *Figure 4–3*

meeting. Her evaluation was based on nontextual considerations, which Thomas Newkirk (1988) identifies as the experience depicted and the evaluation of the experience. Sarah was extending herself beyond the concreteness of the drawing; in fact, her evaluation existed before the drawing.

By first grade, topic selection has become a highly conscious act because students have internalized the question "What are you going to write about next?" Erik was a first grader in a classroom where several of my students were mainstreamed for writing. When I came to work with them, I often talked with Erik, who always had something he wanted to write about. One day in the spring, when he didn't know what to write next, I told him that sometimes when I am stuck, I write down three or four topics. I showed him how I think about each one and decide on the one that interests me most. Erik chose to adopt this suggestion but developed his own book format. When he finished writing it, he called me over to share it. He was excited because this kind of writing, or visual thinking, had been fun and had yielded him a topic (Figure 4–4). Throughout his book he evaluated the topics that came to mind and rejected them because he had already written about them—until he came to Boston. After he had shared his book with his classmate Elizabeth and me, he began to write about Boston.

When Nathan was in first grade, his mother had to be hospitalized for an extended period of time, and he was confused by the whole experience. The day she left he had difficulty saying good-bye to her, so a few days later I asked him if he'd like to write her a letter. He said he didn't know how, he had never written one before. I told him that I would like to write to her too, and we could do our letters together. He wrote the date and greeting according to my example, but he knew enough to write "Dear Mom" rather than "Dear Linda." Nathan was very happy and asked, "Can I put this in one of those things [an envelope]? Can I mail it? She'll like my letter!" At this point we talked about what he wanted to say, and I told him that in a letter it is nice to ask how the other person is and tell the person something about yourself. He proceeded to write the letter in Figure 4–5. It says: "I'm fine, but I hurt my knee. How are you?" As soon as he was finished, Nathan began looking for an envelope.

Even at the earliest stages in the development of a piece of writing, students are thinking critically about the drawings they will make, the experiences they will represent, the topics they will select, and the forms these will take. This critical thinking continues as they begin to draft their pieces of writing.

It was not good enough to talk about a curriculum; the group attempted to demonstrate what was being espoused by providing specific pictures and stories of effective language arts classrooms.

Thinking Throughout the Process   **79**

Erik's Piece   Figure 4–4

A. Humm, hum. What shall I write?
   Hum, hum, hum.

B. What should Erik write?
   I don't know what he should write.
   Neither do I.

C. Why don't you write about planes?
   I already did.
   Oh.

D. I still don't know.

E. Why don't you write about mom or
      dad or your little sister?
   I already did.
   Why didn't you tell me?

F. Oh, I know what to write.
   I'm going to write about Boston.

Figure 4–5 *Nathan's Letter*

June w 198-

DR MOM,
IM FIN B+ I
hrt MI NE
HO r U?
Nathan LOV, XO

Midway Evaluations: Responding to Questions of Process, Content, and Audience During Drafting and Revising

Jason is in the same classroom as Erik, and although he too was not one of my resource room students, I often talked with him about his writing. Once, when I asked him how his writing was going, he said, "Now this page I'm really proud of. Do you know how long it took me to do this page? Three days!" (Figure 4–6). The syntax shows that Jason wrote this page over a period of time. He evaluated his writing through the investment of time he had made. Jason still struggles with letter formation—he had turned his *m*'s right side up because they looked like *w*'s—and spelling, although he used *-ing*, which he had recently learned. I agreed with Jason's evaluation and told him that I certainly could see why he was proud of that page in his book on fishing.

It took Joel, a third grader, one reading period to complete his piece on Halley's Comet (Figure 4–7). He had been "reading" about the comet in the *National Geographic World Magazine* and in every other book either he or I could find. He also talked about his own sightings. I suggested that he write about his experiences so he could share them with others. Two days later he produced his comet piece and shared it with me. I repeated back to Joel the main content of his piece to check his meaning and then asked him what he was going to do next. He said he was going to put it away because it was just to help him remember. Now he wanted to read more. Although I had hoped that Joel might want to develop this piece of writing, I realized that it was a page in a field notebook in his self-selected study of Halley's Comet. He had no reason to revise. He next wrote about Edmund Halley in his effort to use writing to learn.

The outcome of David's piece about his dad was similar (Figure 4–8). It was written like any other piece during writing time, but once David had shared it with me, and I had reflected back what I had heard, he wanted to put it away. I realized that it was a page in a personal journal, and there was no reason to revise.

Amelia, a student in a third-grade classroom in which I was working with some of my mainstreamed students, was writing an essay on nature for a local contest. When she read her piece on flowers to me, I repeated

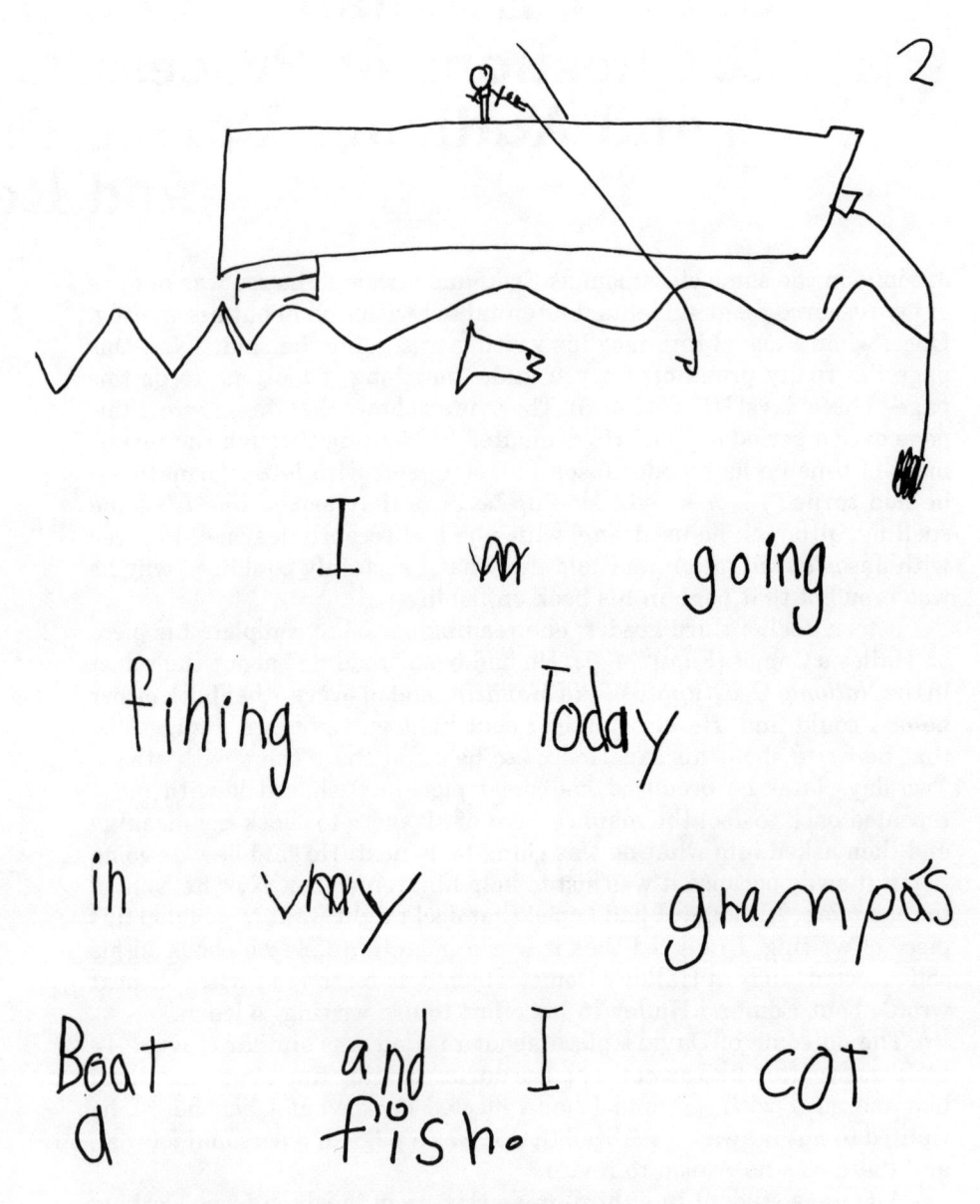

Figure 4–6 Jason's Page

I am going
fihing Today
in my granpas
Boat and I cot
a fish.

I am going fishing today in my grandpa's boat and I caught a fish.

Joel's Piece   Figure 4–7

> Halley's Comet
> Me and my Dad went out my Drivway to sey Halley's comet and we did it wose the briytst thiy in the sciy it wose in the west and it was Down close to the Horizon and it dedt have a tal I sor it mor than to tims.

Halley's Comet
Me and my dad went out my driveway to see Halley's comet and we did. It was the brightest thing in the sky. It was in the west and it was down close to the horizon and it didn't have a tail. I saw it more than two times.

Figure 4–8   *David's Piece*

> about my Dad.
> My DaDDiD a logtime
> agow. I luvd my DaD.
> he Wos nice toawme.
> My DaD Was Strog.
> he Shot his self.
> My mom didit letme
> go to his funrul.
> I was Sad. he is DeD Now

About My Dad
My dad died a long time ago. I loved my dad. He was nice to me. My dad was strong. He shot himself. My mom didn't let me go to his funeral. I was sad. He is dead now.

Thinking Throughout the Process

what I had heard in her piece back to her so that she could listen to its content and sequence. When I repeated her line "picking too many flowers can destroy nature," I asked if she knew of certain flowers that shouldn't be picked at all. She answered, "Lady's slippers! I didn't tell about lady's slippers." There was a pause and she said, "I didn't tell about my favorite flower, bluets. You can pick them. At my grandmother's and great-grandmother's house, the yard is full of bluets." There was another pause and Amelia said, "I'm going to add that to make this really good!"

When Joel read his biographical sketch of his grandfather (Figure 4–9), I asked him about the statements "He had four planes" and "he stopped flying in 1985," because I doubted their validity. Joel had been my student for five years, and I knew his family very well. His piece went through his revision as well as editing by his classroom teacher, but those statements did not change until he was writing his final copy. He came over to me and, referring to the statement about the four planes, said, "Maybe I should leave that out. I want this to be right. I can't check with my grampy. He went to Florida yesterday." I also noticed that Joel had changed 1985 to 1945 in his effort to validate his writing.

B.J. came to me from a special school when he was in third grade. Although he was capable of writing, B.J. had never written much other than his name and the date or to practice handwriting because the curriculum did not provide for it. He began writing by drawing and labeling and moved rapidly to expanded text. By January, I was able to move him back to the classroom for reading and writing and was there to support him. He wrote a poem about the space shuttle disaster to express how he was feeling (Figure 4–10). After I had reflected back what I had heard in the poem, I asked him about how he had written it. I wondered if his use of the acrostic was conscious; I had taught it to him at Christmas time in an attempt to interest him in writing poetry—despite its formulaic approach. He thought hard for a few minutes and then said, "I thought about each line before I wrote it down. Then I wrote it out and thought about the next line." I asked, "Did you do anything else?" He answered, "When it was all done, I read it over to see if it showed all my feelings. That was when I added 'and a lot of puzzles,' because they can't figure out what caused it. Then it had all my feelings." What B.J. didn't consciously realize was that one of his lines was inspired by one of the lines in John Gillespie Magee's "High Flight": "Put out my hand and touched the face of God." B.J. added his poem to a bulletin board dedicated to the astronauts.

Questions about audience don't have much effect on kindergartners, but I begin to ask them anyway. When Daniel was working on his book about his baby brother, Shawn (Figure 4–11), I asked him who might be

Figure 4–9   *Joel's Biographical Sketch*

Lewis Johnson

My grampy, Lewis Johnson was born in Portland in 1926. He worked in a shipyard before he went in the service. He went into the Army Air Corps, and that is where he learned how to fly. He started flying in 1945 and stopped flying in 1945. He was in World War II. After the war he was a boatbuilder and then built his own boat. He had two children: Larry and Linda. He got married in 1946 to Frances Childs. They built their own hose.

B. J.'s Poem   Figure 4–10

Space Shuttle

School teacher is ready,
people look happy to see 7 people go up in space,
astronauts were going to learn about Halley's Comet.
challenger went up,
exploded in the air and a lot of puzzles.

Sad Feelings happening now,
high school kids feel the pain in them,
up to see God to touch hands.
time to go on with the space program,
tv shows keep showing all around,
let people think back about the happy things,
every one did feel the pain in them.

By B.J.
3rd Grade

Teachers Telling Their Stories

Figure 4–11   *Daniel's Book*

MIBABEBOOK

SHAUN·CROLEING

SHAUNCLIMEING UNTHETABAL

SHAUN·PLEING THE·LEP

A. Shawn crawling

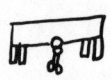

B. Shawn climbing on the table

C. Shawn pulling the lamp

SHAUNPECE·ING IPTHE·LETL·PES·AF DRT

SHAUNSICLI·ING HESBADAL

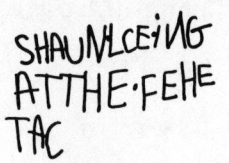

SHAUNLCEING ATTHE·FEHE TAC

D. Shawn picking up little pieces of dirt

E. Shawn sucking his bottle

F. Shawn looking at the fish tank

interested in reading it. Daniel blinked and didn't reply, so I moved on. When Daniel finished writing his book a day later, he brought it over to me and announced, "This book is great. It's about Shawn!" I blinked in surprise because it was unusual for Daniel to make such strong statements, even though his voice was quiet and controlled. He then added, "My parents want to see it. I told them all about it." Daniel proceeded to write a whole series of books about his family: Michael (his older brother), Daddy, Mommy, Nana, and Grampy. At the end of the series, Daniel interviewed me with the kind of questions I often used on him.

Daniel: How did I get so good at writing?
S: What do you think?
D: I don't know.
S: I think it is because you write all the time. You practice a lot.
D: I think I do pretty good. [*Daniel paused and then brought up another concern.*] I got to learn to read. I can read the easy books you taught me [predictable books], but I can't read other books I try to read [unfamiliar].

Self-evaluations during the actual writing of a piece usually occur as the student looks over, reads, or otherwise reflects on the writing. For some students the process—the investment of time, how a piece is written, or whom it is for—is significant. For others, content—its significance, its completeness, or its validity—is most important. Revisions in content do or do not occur, depending on the students' evaluation. In conferences, we can help students think through their writing, but their revisualizing of it depends on their evaluation of what they have already written.

End Point Evaluations: Editing and Publishing Decisions

The editing/publishing conference with primary students is a rich time for self-evaluation. When my students complete five or so drafted booklets, they select what they consider to be their best story to be typed with conventional spelling and other forms and bound in an attractive cover. They illustrate the book and share it with the class and their families; then it is put on display in the classroom. There are many other forms of publication, but this is the type referred to in this section.

When I asked Stephanie, who is Erik and Jason's first grade classmate, why she chose to publish "My Friends," she answered, "I like this one. I like making people. Rae publishes her books on people, and she teaches me how to draw. Her people books are my favorites. Rae draws people good. Her mother is an artist."

Anticipating my question about what he would like to publish, Bryan, a first grader, had already made his decision. When I asked him why he had chosen this particular piece (Figure 4–12), he replied, "Well, I like drawing pumpkins; it's all about pumpkins. See, it says [*and he read*], 'Pumpkin, pumpkin, pumpkin, pumpkin, pumpkin.'" Then he paused as he suddenly realized that the text was the same for each picture and added, "Every one is doing something different!" He showed me the pictures and told me about them. Although I had been suggesting to Bryan that he could write a book on a single topic since last spring, this was the first time he had done so; since then I have "nudged" him—Mary Ellen Giacobbe's word for consistent suggesting—to write about the differences among the pictures.

William, a first grader, had a very difficult time last spring choosing which book to publish. He liked two of them, "Bigfoot" and "André," equally well. "Bigfoot" had his friends in it, and "André," he said, was "good and funny." I remembered when William had shared "André" with the group. Everyone who had been to see the famous seal shared their experiences, and we had all laughed a lot together. I could see what William meant, so I published both books.

Some students choose to publish a particular book because they have achieved control over conventions. Nathan chose to publish his book about the YMCA because he liked the Y and because the book had sentences with periods. I had been "nudging" him toward sentences for a long time and had taught him the use of the period when he wrote the Y book.

During an editing conference, after I had taught Joel to put in the addresses on a business letter (Figure 4–13), he looked at me and said, "Now I know why I didn't get anything from that cereal company. I didn't put on any addresses." (He was referring to when he had written a letter at home asking for free materials.) When he got his poster on Halley's Comet, he came and told me that it had arrived and that he was glad he did his letter "right."

Of course, control over conventions is cause for self-evaluation at any time. Donnie showed me that he knew how to write "cb" for *cub* rather than "kb" because *car* and *cabin* sound like *k* but use *c* in spelling (Figure 4–14). James brought over a page in his book, which he read as "Me bowling," and remarked, "I sounded it out all by myself!"

When young children are asked to select and finalize a piece of writing

Thinking Throughout the Process

Bryan's Book — *Figure 4–12*

Figure 4–13   Joel's Letter

> Boothbay Reg. Elem. Sch
> Boothbay Harbor, Maine 04538
> February 4, 1986
>
> The Ball Corporation
> Aerospace Systems Division
> Comet Halley poster, 5020-2
> P.O. Box 1062, Boulder, Colorado 80306
>
> Dear Sir or Madam:
> please can you get me a poster about Halley's Comet from National Geographic World, and more information? I've been Reading about Halley's Comet. Thank you For sending it.
>
> Sincerely
> Joel Johnson

Thinking Throughout the Process 93

Donnie's Piece   *Figure 4–14*

BAAS   DoNNIE ~~KB~~ CB

bears cub

by publishing it, they are evaluating the product, what Thomas Hilger calls "summing up." For some, it is the illustrated part of the piece that makes it best; for others, it is the written text. For still others, especially young children, it is the control over conventions that marks their best. Their reasons will shift as their perception about what is good shifts, and in accordance with what they are trying to do, but two that remain fairly constant are their liking for the subject and the response the writing brings from others.

Evaluation, Responsibility, and Growth

Student self-evaluation is a natural part of writing and responding. Evaluation occurs at all stages of the writing process, and it is crucial to the writer's engagement in the same piece or to the pursuit of the same subject in different pieces. Besides engagement, these evaluations are essential for two other reasons: they give the writer control and ownership over the writing, and they provide the basis for teaching—for planning and assessing teacher response. I cannot imagine how I could teach students without having these "windows on their minds."

For a long time, a part of me thought that the "real" evaluation must occur at the final stages of writing and that it was my responsibility. I even used to feel a little bit guilty about my students' involvement, particularly because some of the teachers walked around armed with grade books and always seemed to know what was A, B, C, or D without any input from their students. Although I knew that evaluation is more complex than that and believed that ultimately the responsibility for it is with the writer, I still thought I had to be in charge.

Linda Rief, middle school teacher from Oyster River School in Durham, New Hampshire, convinced me that it is as necessary for kids to have control over evaluation as it is for them to have control over topic choice. In 1980, when I first heard that kids were choosing their own topics, I thought it was heresy, but my students quickly showed me how valid it was. And as a result of researching students' self-evaluation and uncovering my own assumptions, I have recognized that *all evaluations, at all stages of the process, are real evaluations*. I know that I play a part in the process, but I do not control it.

> ...each of us in his or her own way harped on the centrality of the child in any discussion of what English studies should be or how English should be taught.

Getting down what kids say and do in evaluating their writing as well as what others say and do that affects their evaluations is a challenge. Stepping outside myself and watching what we do together is a bigger challenge. In tracing her own development as a teacher-researcher, Nancie Atwell has said that she first conducted research to confirm her beliefs and theories. Second, she emphasized herself less and instead followed what her kids did in their literary endeavors. Third, she watched what she and her students did collaboratively as they found ways to query and form theories together. By looking at writing samples and at the responses and behaviors of both my students and myself, I have attempted that third stage of teacher research. In teaching, I will continue to untangle the web of interactive response by doing research. The more closely I look at self-evaluation, the more I learn about my teaching and the more my students learn about their writing.

REFERENCES

Atwell, Nancie. 1986. "A More Principled Practice: The Teacher Researcher." Speech, "New Directions in Composition Scholarship," University of New Hampshire, Durham, N.H. October.

Genishi, Celia, and Anne Haas Dyson. 1985. *Language Assessment in Early Years*. Norwood, N.J.: Ablex.

Graves, Donald. 1985. "All Children Can Write." *Learning Disabilities Focus* 1:36–43.

Hilgers, Thomas. 1986a. "How Children Change as Critical Evaluators of Writing: Four Three-Year Case Studies." *Research in the Teaching of English* 20:36–55.

———. 1986b. "Writer's Evaluations of Writing: A Comparison of Criteria Used by Primary-School and College Students." Speech, "New Directions in Composition Scholarship," University of New Hampshire, Durham, N.H. October.

Newkirk, Thomas. 1988. "Young Writers as Critical Readers." In *Understanding Writing: Ways of Observing, Learning, and Teaching*, ed. Thomas Newkirk and Nancie Atwell. 2d. ed. Portsmouth, N.H.: Heinemann.

Stires, Susan. 1983a. "Disabled Writers: A Positive Approach." In *Teaching All the Children to Write*, ed. James Collins. Buffalo, N.Y.: New York State English Council.

———. 1983b. "Real Audiences and Contexts for LD Writers." *Academic Therapy* 18:561–68.

5

Writing What They Read
Reflections on Literature and Child Writers
FREDRICK R. BURTON

> *The education of a gardener is not a process that fits easily into a classroom or can be ferreted out of books during the falls and winters of four short years. It takes as many years as you have to give and then some. The reason, of course, is that formal knowledge is only one small ingredient of what is a complex concoction. Good gardeners, like their gardens, are distilled from a slow brew of long experience and personal alchemy.*
> (Cooper 1985, 2)

Things had come to a crisis. It seemed such a short time since I had left my teaching position in an elementary school on the plains of Wyoming. I had just spent three academically rewarding years as a teaching and research associate studying language arts and children's literature at Ohio State University. Although I had been exposed to a great deal of

> ...a distinctive characteristic of the Coalition Conference was the voice of the classroom teacher....

formal knowledge, I felt that something was missing. I was becoming less interested in research "findings" and more interested in personal meaning. After all, it is personal meaning acquired through action, reflection, and deliberation as one lives through experiences with children—not "findings"—that ultimately makes a difference.

It was at this point that I decided to leave the university and take a position in a public alternative elementary school, one grounded in Deweyan philosophy, as a teacher of a combination class of third and fourth graders. My university advisers graciously agreed to allow me to do my doctoral research *as* a teacher rather than *on* a teacher. And so for the next two years I systematically explored the connections between the composing processes of children and their literary experiences in my classroom. Specifically, I wanted to know how children used literature *for their own purposes* as writers.

As I explored the connection between children's writing and their literary experiences, a major theme began to surface throughout their work. I observed child writers *borrowing and improvising* on their literary knowledge in a variety of ways. The borrowing and improvising seemed to occur both tacitly and consciously. I will discuss the ways in which children borrow and improve on: 1) literary language patterns; 2) literary formats; and 3) various elements of literature itself. My sources are their writing and a personal journal in which I recorded day-to-day thoughts on teaching and reflected on potential meanings of a child's work and directions I might take.

Language Patterns

Child writers borrowed and improvised on the language of literature. By language patterns I am referring to an author's use of text at the *word* and *phrase* levels. Children produced written compositions that were structurally or rhythmically similar to an author's text. The borrowing was most common in the fiction they wrote but was also apparent in their informational writing.

The sounds, rhythm, and syntax of language were points of pleasure for many of the children. This was especially true for children like Tom.

> *2/27 Tom approached Sherry today and quoted her writing (actually paraphrased it). He chose the first line of her "Christmas Presents" story ("Sue Ellen Parkins, did you hear me?").*

> *2/28   Tom approached me during Sustained Silent Reading time and asked if he could make a list of unusual words he was finding in the books he was reading to himself.*

This interest in the language of literature was often connected to hearing it during read-aloud time, a classroom event that occurred for thirty to forty-five minutes each day.

> *4/10   Sherry (as well as a couple of others) has been keeping her own list of special words. She handed it to me yesterday after read-aloud. So far she has: "slippings and drippings," "slashes and gashes," and "bumpings and jumpings." All of these are rhyming phrases uttered by Gurgi, a character in our current read-aloud book,* The Black Cauldron. *Most of the class has delighted in the dialogue and seems especially pleased with Gurgi's use of language.*

Ann's story "The Green Book Part II" was begun the day I finished reading Walsh's science fiction novelette, *The Green Book*. Her interest in this story illustrates the power that a single word can have for a child.

> *1/23   After I asked for ways to extend* The Green Book, *Ann suggested writing a part 2 to it. She was one of the first in the class to borrow my copy. At first, I thought she just wanted to know some of the names of characters—perhaps in order to spell them correctly.*
>
> *Later, she went back to the book again to try to find out what the people on the planet "Shine" had called the bread that they had tried to make from the glass-like grains of wheat. Robert told her they called them pancakes, but she wasn't satisfied with that. I honestly tried to remember, but she was dissatisfied that my suggestions (e.g., brown bread) were only guesses. She wanted authenticity. Finally, after looking through the book for several minutes, she found the word—"panbread."*

Although she only used the word "panbread" once in her story, it was clearly important to her. As I noted in my reflective observations, I think its importance was the result of her interest in authenticity. Because her story was a "Part II," using a word from the book allowed her to preserve some of the original content of Walsh's book. Her determination to get the "right" word, even if it meant interrupting her composing while searching the pages of the original book for several minutes, was not an uncommon practice among the other children as well.

"Panbread" is a rather ordinary word. In their own stories children were more likely to choose words that were in some way unique, words that sounded interesting or were relevant.

Like Ann, Mary became interested in some words from a read-aloud book. She then proceeded to insert these words into the middle of "The Pegasus That Wanted a Horn," a story that she had started on April 1. On May 1, midway through her story, she wrote:

> *The next day they started off.*
> *"Off we go!"*
> *"Oh let's have breakfast first."*
> *"OK."*
> *"Yummy, yummy this is good. What is it?"*
> *"It's a snuzcumber."*
> *"Yuck, that's sick," said Mercury.*
> *"Want a drink?"*
> *"OK."*
> *"Have a drink."*
> *"Yum, what's this?"*
> *"Frogskotll."*
> *"Oh no and what was that wiener looking thing?"*
> *"A snozcumber."*
> *"And that icky looking drink that gives you wizpoppers and not burpers?"*
> *"It's a snozcumber and frogskotll."*
> *"Oh, well let's go!" said Athena.*
> *"OK."*
> *Off they go. Meanwhile, Venus was struggling to stay alive when suddenly she heard a familiar voice. It was Athena.*
> *"Mommy, mommy, she yelled, Athena my darling you have found me."*
> *"Of course we have. That's what I wanted to do."*

Commenting in my reflective observations, I noted:

> 5/1 Once again, another read-aloud book is coming into play—this time Dahl's The B.F.G., a book my substitute teacher read aloud all last week. Mary uses words

> *from* The B.F.G. *like "snuzcumber" (food), "frogskotll" (drink), and "wizpopper" (passing gas). At this point Mary's story appears to have taken a detour. It is her* joy in Dahl's nonsense words and his story that appear to be affecting *her* plot which has to do with Athena's quest for her lost mother.... She has found a way to sneak and weave this joy into her story. She makes it fit by having her characters stop *as an afterthought* in her excerpt on 5/1.

In contrast to Ann's concern with authenticity, Mary is taken with the words for their own sake. Their sounds and the humorous context in which Dahl uses them motivate her borrowing. She writes these words willingly, even at the expense of the rhythm of her storyline. She is working her delight in nonsense words into her story.

While Ann was concerned with the authenticity that a word borrowed from a story would give her own writing and Mary was exclusively interested in words *as* words, other child writers like Jackie and Kathy were clearly concerned with both.

During the early stages of an eight-week class study on the Middle Ages, I had read aloud De Angeli's *The Door in the Wall*, a novel set in the fourteenth century that centers around the struggles of a nobleman's crippled son to find his place in medieval society. As the class study unfolded, children chose areas of medieval life to study. Jackie and Kathy became interested in the social classes of the period. Although I had hoped that they would focus their attention on the social discrepancies and hardships of the peasantry, they were primarily interested in the nobility.

It was at this point that I decided to introduce them to Lasker's *Merry Ever After*, a picture book comparing the weddings of couples from the noble *and* the peasant classes. The subject of this book gave them the idea of spinning a fantasy in which they were both princesses about to be married. They decided to begin writing a series of letters to each other from the point of view of the princesses. An excerpt from their imaginary correspondence follows:

> *Dear Princess Olivia,*
> *It tis getting boring around the palace. I have not heard from thou in such a long time. Where have you been? I have been afraid you were hurt. How is thou brother O'Patrick?*
>
> *Sincerely,*
> *Princess O'Kate*

> *Dear Princess O'Kate,*
> *Ivan got your letter yesterday. I am fine. How art you? I have been around the palace. Well, it is a sad story. O'Patrick was playing outside and he hit his head on a pole and fell in the well and got himself a bad cold.*
> *Sincerely,*
Olivia

> *Princess Olivia,*
> *I'm so sorry your brother was hurt. Give thou brother my care. A funny thing happened to me at the market. Old Cousin O'Taran is getting married to the lady who runs the market.*
> *Sincerely,*
O'Kate

Although the content of this series of letters was influenced by Lasker's *Merry Ever After*, the language patterns more accurately reflect the language of De Angeli's *A Door in the Wall*, as this excerpt shows:

> *"Come, my son. Doth thy father stop to say 'I cannot go into battle for my King because arrows are sharp'? Off with thy clothes, I say, else thou'lt lose the strength and skill thou hast begun to have. 'Tis a long way from freezing." While he spoke he lifted Robin down and helped him to undress and go into the river. (54)*

At the word level, "thou," "tis," and "art" give the letters of Jackie and Kathy a medieval flavor that is exactly like that in De Angeli's novel. The children have assimilated these words into their existing language patterns.

Literary Formats

Children borrowed and improvised on a book's literary format. By the literary format of a book, I mean its typography, illustrations, and the way its text and illustrations are organized. In this definition I am also including the more taken-for-granted components of format, such as the title page, dedication page, jacket flap, jacket cover, and the "about the author" page. Children used the literary format of a text as a guide in shaping their own piece of writing.

At times, they focused on very specific aspects of format. For example, some children were observed reading the "about the author" page on the jacket flap of books. This was not surprising since the children's intention in doing so was obvious—to get ideas for writing "about the author" pages for their own books. The format of the typical "about the author" page is usually a short biographical statement or a comment about the process of creating the book itself (e.g., the media used to do the illustrations). The following example is taken from a book by Peter Parnall, a noted children's illustrator and author.

> **About the Author (excerpts from *Alfalfa Hill*)**
> *Peter Parnall has always loved the land and the creatures that inhabit it. During part of his childhood he lived in a desert, where there were more wild things than children for playmates....In addition to writing and illustrating, he designs trademarks, and teaches at Lafayette College.*

The matter-of-fact content and style of the children's "about the author" writing reflect this format.

> **About the Author (from *Wild Sail*)**
> *Peter Yates is ten years old. He has done two other books,* Fables *and* Wild Sail. Wild Sail *is the first book in this series. He is working on another book called* Destiny. *He plays soccer, baseball, and football. His favorite vacation spot is Colorado.*

> **About the Author (from *Joe and the Germs*)**
> *Keith Smith is ten years old. He likes gymnastics. He has one brother named Sean. Keith has written this book for his enjoyment and yours.*

> **About the Author (from *Tom and His Muscles*)**
> *Charles Richards is ten years old and is in the fourth grade at Barrington Elementary School in Upper Arlington, Ohio. Charles lives with his father, mother and twelve year old sister. He likes to play sports. His favor-*

ite is football followed by baseball. Charles can also be found in a serious game of chess or checkers. He has a hamster and a cat.

Children rarely borrowed and improvised on literary formats in a piecemeal fashion. Instead, they usually responded to more than one aspect of format—e.g., how the placement of text and illustrations worked together as a whole. I believe that this type of borrowing and improvising was also a result of my occasional attempts to call attention to how the components of format worked in a book.

Many of today's informational books for children have unique formats. During a class study of "The Human Body," I shared and displayed in the classroom several informational books that presented their topics in various formats (e.g., Holling's *Paddle-to-the-Sea*, Macaulay's *Castle*, McGovern's *...If You Lived With the Sioux Indians*, Musgrove's *Ashanti to Zulu*, de Paola's *Charlie Needs a New Cloak*, Simon's *Animal Fact/Animal Fable*, Hoft's *Biography of a Rhino*, George's *All Upon a Sidewalk*, and Brady's *Wildmouse*). Afterwards, I suggested to the children that they might want to present their own topics in their human body project using a format other than the typical school report. Most of them did.

Sherry's written composition illustrates just how children used a book's format in their writing. Sherry had spent several weeks making notes from informational books on the human eye. She became intrigued with Simon's *Animal Fact/Animal Fable*, which is an interesting variation on the question-and-answer format. In *Animal Fact/Animal Fable*, Simon presents a collection of beliefs about animals as a guessing game. For example, on one page the following statement appears:

Camels store water in their humps.

After the reader guesses whether or not the statement is a fact or fable, he or she turns the page to find the explanation:

FABLE. A camel's hump does not hold water, it stores fat. The stored fat is used for energy when the camel doesn't get enough food. But camels go for days or even weeks without drinking water. Their woolly coats keep out the heat of the direct sunlight. The wool also keeps them from sweating and losing water too rapidly. A camel's body is just right for living in a hot and dry place.

Writing What They Read

Sherry chose to use Simon's format to present the information she had gathered on the human eye. Her own book, *Eye Fact/Eye Fable*, is excerpted below.

> *Your pupil is behind your cornea.*
> FACT OR FABLE?
> *(turn page)*
>
> FACT: *Your pupil is a hole in the middle of the iris. The cornea is a tough clear shield protecting and letting light into the pupil.*
>
> *Your iris does not control the amount of light going into the pupil.*
> FACT OR FABLE?
> *(turn page)*
>
> FABLE: *Your iris does control the amount of light going into the pupil. In the dark, the iris lets more light into the pupil and where it is light it lets less light into the pupil.*
>
> *Your eye is not tough, it is soft.*
> FACT OR FABLE?
> *(turn page)*
>
> FABLE: *The white part of your eye is called the sclera. It is very tough. It protects the other parts of your eye and most of the other parts are pretty tough too.*
>
> *The cornea is the colored part of your eye.*
> FACT OR FABLE?
> *(turn page)*
>
> FABLE: *The iris is the colored part of your eye. It can be blue, green, brown, and if you are an albino, it can even be pinkish.*

The format of Simon's book appeared to support Sherry's writing process in that it allowed her to organize the numerous notes she had accumulated over the weeks. Although she has borrowed the format, the writing is hers alone. After reviewing Sherry's writing much later, I confirmed the improvisational character of her "Eye Fact/Eye Fable."

> *11/7/84 Obviously, Sherry has mastered the use of the guessing game structure. Even more impressive is the fact that she has worked hard to present the information in her own way, avoiding the trap of lifting entire sections from other sources.*

Borrowing from Traditional Literary Elements

A broader category that helped me explore some of the literary links in children's writing involved the traditional criteria by which literature is evaluated. These traditional elements include characterization, plot, setting, theme, style, and tone. Children were observed borrowing these basic elements of literature and improvising on them in a variety of ways and for a range of purposes. Most of this borrowing involved more than one literary element. At times the influences were very direct and related to a specific book. At other times they were more diffuse in that children's use of these elements occurred on a more abstract level.

Writing a "Part II" to a book they had previously read or heard appealed to many of the children. However, such stories, rather than merely being copies of the original text, were personal versions that varied with the intentions of the children.

Two versions of Walsh's *The Green Book* serve as examples. The first is an unfinished one by Ann.

> **The Green Book, Part II**
> (*author's note: read* The Green Book *by Jill Walsh before you read this book*)
>
> *After Father finished Patty's book, we all went back to our cabins to talk about what we thought of it. By this time, Patty had fallen asleep in Father's lap. He said, "How did she do it in such detail?"*
>
> *"I guess we all have something to think about," said Sara.*
>
> *"Well, we better hit the sack," said Joel.*
>
> *"Good idea," agreed Father.*

> *The next morning we had panbread for breakfast again. Then the grownups had a meeting about a library. Father said he would not let the library have his book of gadgets. "I will not put my book in a library for anything," he said. When he got home he hid the book in case Malcom or the guide came to look for it while he wasn't home.*
>
> *The next day, Patty and Joe went to catch more jelly fish for the camp to use for lamps. They used thin pieces of wood for poles and some string from the ship for a line. They must have caught at least 100 because they took ten trips to the shore before they stopped.*
>
> *[Joel asked] "Dad can I borrow your book of technology?"*
> *"Yes, but return it."*
> *(later)*
> *"Hey Joel, can I borrow that book?"*
> *"Alright Malcom, I'll ask my dad."*
> *"No, I'll tell him. Thanks."*

Over the next three weeks, Ann met with me in writing conferences to share and discuss her story.

> *1/23 ... Ann's story quickly picks up where the other left off—i.e., from the discovery that Patty's book was filled up with words. After her characters briefly admire the detail of Patty's book, they decide it's time for bed. It was at this point that Ann shared with me that she was stuck.*
>
> *At times, I just sympathize with kids and say—"yes, being stuck is a normal problem that writers have." But today, I helped Ann to think about what might happen next. I asked her what the characters might do in order to build a society (after first telling her that her sentence that puts her characters to bed makes it logical to start—"and the next day they...."). She responded by saying that "I'd first have them build a library."*
>
> *Although at the time I didn't think much about this idea, it seems more important now and I wished I had pursued it with Ann. After all, the role of books was an important theme in the story. Books were a way to entertain, record culture, and learn in Walsh's novel.*

> *1/29 Ann has been dividing her time between working on "The Green Book, Part II" and her collaborative piece with Sandy called "Me and Monique."... Ann continues her "Green Book" story with the building of a library which, after our writing conference today, she decided would be important to the new society. Indeed, that was of major importance to the new society in Walsh's book. It was also a major theme of the book—i.e., the importance of books/stories to improve, enrich, and sustain our lives.*
>
> *Ann has also set up a conflict in the plot—i.e., Father refuses to contribute his book on technology to the group library.... Ann has taken the idea of Father's clinging attitude toward his book into her own story. Clearly, she has understood this element of Father's character.*

Ann has understood two of the themes in Walsh's *The Green Book*: 1) the importance of stories to society, and 2) the tension between the needs of the individual and those of the larger society. Her story revolves around these two themes along with her understanding of Father's character. I hoped that Ann would continue with this story, but instead, she filed her work in her writing folder and began an autobiography entitled "The First Two Lives of Ann Burns" (the idea of this title was taken from a book she had begun reading, *The First Two Lives of Lukas Kasha*, by Alexander).

While Ann's story preserves the serious tone of Walsh's book, the underlying intent of Sherry and Sally's story, "The Green Book: Their Adventures on Shine," is quite different.

> **The Green Book: Their Adventures on Shine**
> By Sherry and Sally
> *Father finished reading Patty's book. The children went to play hopskotch while their parents had a discussion about Patty's book. Malcom said, "I don't see how Patty could do her book in such detail." "Yes, I know. She's such a wonderful child," Father bragged.*
>
> *Meanwhile, Patty and Jason were having a fight about who got to stand on which boulder. Patty said, "I want that pink and purple polk-a-doted one." "So...do ...I," complained Jason.*

Suddenly, Patty noticed the pink and purple one had disappeared. Then Patty saw it had reappeared and burped at her.

"Burrrrp," burped the Boulder. Then the Boulder said, "Welcome to the fireworks show of 1988 contributed by the Mouth People. Then the Boulder hollered, "And here they are." All of the Boulders burst into the sky and out came beautiful purple, pink, and green Mouth People.

Suddenly Patty remembered that she had some Tree Candy in her pocket. Little did she know that Mouth People could read minds. Suddenly the pink, purple, and green swarm swooped down and pulled her pants off to get the Tree Candy out of her pockets. Luckily, Patty had long johns on.

"Help, help," screamed Patty. Patty looked at Jason who was now standing on the pink and purple boulder having a laughing fit. Then that boulder blew up like the other boulders. Jason was thrown all the way to the pond.

Then Patty remembered that she had the Tree Candy in her pocket. Oh no, the Mouth People heard her. So she pushed Jason where she had been standing while she hid behind the boulder. The Mouth People couldn't see very well, so they attacked Jason thinking that it was Patty.

Meanwhile, Patty had run home to get another pair of pants on. "Father, the Mouth People are very mean. They read minds and pull off pants."

"Ha, ha, looks like we'll have to wear suspender's from now on."

"Daddy, cried Patty, that's not funny. If we wear suspenders, when they pull off our pants they would snap back and hurt us."

"Well then I can't help you."

Patty ran into her room and put on her corduroy jeans, but this time she wore shorts underneath her pants. Right then Father rushed into her room. "Patty this is no joke. Shine is going to blow up. We need fuel, can we burn you up?"

"Daddy."

"Just kidding. We need your help to get jelly fish for fuel."

"OK daddy. I'll go help right away. Hey, how much time till we leave?"

"Till tomorrow morning."

"Oh no."

The next day they packed up their stuff and put it on their spaceship. They brought their books, clothes, lots of panbread, and lots of Tree Candy. At about 2:00 pm, they took off. Three years later, they found themselves on the planet Dull. Everybody knew, except for Patty, that secretly she had brought along another book besides the Green Book. Because she thought she might want to write about something else, she brought: THE RED BOOK.

The End

In the spirit of National Lampoon's satire on the Tolkien fantasy trilogy, *Bored of the Rings*, Sherry and Sally have used various elements of Walsh's book in order to attempt their own irreverent version. They satirized the book's serious tone (having the girl losing her pants in a crisis), its characters (using Mouth People instead of Moth People), plot events (the quiet solemnity of the Moth People emerging from the boulders in the original is turned into a staged fireworks event in which the Mouth People respond by burping), and setting (going from the planet "Shine" to the planet "Dull").

In both Ann's "The Green Book, Part II" and Sherry's and Sally's "The Green Book: Their Adventures on Shine," the authors have spent time revisiting and discussing the original version. Furthermore, although in both stories the authors have borrowed various literary elements from Walsh's book, as a result of their varying intentions, each version is distinct from the other.

Borrowing and improvising on literary elements *specific to a genre* also occurred. This was particularly true of the folklore genre. For example, this was the case in Mary and Sally's "The Awesome Little Woman" and Alan's "Willy T," which served as modern versions of Mosel's Japanese tale *The Funny Little Woman* and Bawden's *William Tell*, respectively. However, Peter's book, *Fables*, was perhaps the clearest example of this phenomenon.

When asked about the source of his story ideas, Peter, a quiet nine-year-old boy, explained that "they just come from my head." However, in reading Peter's written work throughout the year, one is struck by its literary sophistication.

Writing What They Read

In September, three selections from Lobel's *Fables* were read aloud to the entire class. The children were then invited to try writing their own fable during the next few writing times. No one did. A copy of the book was then put on display.

A few days later, Peter began to read the display copy on his own. He explained how he had read Aesop's fables during the previous school year. It seemed that Lobel's *Fables* had rekindled this interest, since throughout the next five weeks Peter wrote a total of seven fables. Here are five of them:

> *One day a bull feeling both strong and mean came down into the valley. To his surprise, there was another bull down there looking as strong and mean as he. They challenged each other to a fight. They killed each other and neither of them carried on a happy life.*
>
> *Moral: You can't win against an equally equipped opponent.*
>
> *There once was a greedy pig who got up one morning before his brothers and sisters. Seeing their food tray filled, he ran over to eat it up before his brothers and sisters awoke. Soon he was done and stuck in the food tray. He was too fat to get out, so for the rest of that day he was stuck in that position.*
>
> *Moral: Greediness never leads to happiness.*
>
> *Today was mother horse's birthday party and there was a big celebration. Mother horse got presents of all kinds. Soon the news spread to the bear. Hearing this, the bear cleaned himself and filled two whole jars of honey for mother horse. When Mr. Bear got to the party everybody ran away thinking that he had come to eat them up.*
>
> *Moral: Things aren't always what they seem.*
>
> *One day a little lamb's mother gave the little lamb 25 coins of 25 cents to give to the teacher. On the way to school she lost the coins and couldn't seem to find them. The teacher, expecting coins asked, "What happened to them?" But the little lamb said, "One of the students took them," not wanting to admit she had lost them. The truth finally came out in the end. The teacher put the lit-*

tle lamb in the corner, not because she had lost the coins but because she had lied.
Moral: You get a bad image when you lie.

One day a friendly rabbit was hopping down the dirt trail when he met a mean looking porcupine. The rabbit joyfully said, "Hello." But in return the porcupine just stuck him with a quill. The rabbit, in pain, just limped home.
Moral: Happiness can't be found in everyone.

Fables are deceptively simple. An abstract moral must emerge from a concise interplay of story elements. Obviously, Peter has borrowed the conventional elements that make up a fable. The characters are animals that most often remain nameless. Plot and setting are described with economy in mind, as are dialogue and the final moral. As he wrote, Peter sometimes reread selections from Lobel's *Fables*; however, like Lobel, Peter's final written products are fresh creations and are uniquely his own.

Reflections on the Literature–Writing Relationship

...research and instruction must...inform each other.

Because I believe good research is "re-searching" one's experience, I have pulled together some of the "potential meaning" of my teaching and my observations of child writers and their literary experiences.

1. *Borrowing and improvising is a thinking strategy that children use to create text.* This process of borrowing and improvising is an important one for children in their overall development as writers and appears to be something that human beings generally do when they create works of art. Actors study the idiosyncracies of fellow actors. Painters are influenced by the techniques and styles of other painters. Musicians embrace and expand upon the compositions of other musicians. Yet all of these artists create works that stand on their own.

Writers are no exception. They, too, are influenced by the works of other writers. In an article entitled "How I Wrote 'The Name of the Rose,'"

Eco (1984) describes how he used the literary works of others to create his own story:

> I set about reading or rereading medieval chroniclers, to acquire their rhythm and their innocence. They would speak for me, and I would be freed from suspicion. Freed from suspicion, but not from the echoes of intertextuality. Thus I rediscovered what writers have always known (and have told us again and again): books always speak of other books, and every story tells a story that has already been told. Homer knew this, and Ariosto knew this, not to mention Rabelais and Cervantes. (35).

Although borrowing and improvising is a thinking strategy used by human beings as they create works of art, in the context of this study it was a *writing process* strategy. Children's use of this strategy began to illustrate for me in a concrete way what Yolen (1981), referring to the interrelatedness of all literature, meant by the phrase "stories lean on stories." The more I observed children, the more evidence I accumulated depicting how their stories and informational writing leaned on the kinds of experiences they were having with literature.

All of this points to the idea that child writers borrow and improvise in much the same way that adult artists do. As children borrow from and improvise on stories they read and hear, they use their literary heritage to explore and experiment while at the same time using its structures to create written compositions that they alone truly possess.

2. *Children's literature is a necessary component of the writing context.* Just as children emerge as competent readers within a classroom community of readers, child writers emerge within a community of writers. A community of writers includes not only other children who perceive themselves as authors, but also the larger literary community of professional writers and the body of literature they have collected or created. Tolkien (1965) has referred to the collection of existing stories as a "Pot of Soup" and "Cauldron of Story" to which other writers continually add and from which they draw.

Expanding on Tolkien's metaphor, Alexander (1971) states:

> The pot holds a rich and fascinating kind of mythological minestrone. Almost everything has gone into it and almost anything is likely to come out of it: morsels of real history spiced—and spliced—with imaginary his-

> *tory, fact and fancy, daydreams and nightmares. It is as inexhaustible as those legendary vessels that could never be emptied.*
>
> *Among the most nourishing bits and pieces we can scoop out of the pot are whole assortments of characters, events, and situations that occur again and again in one form or another throughout much of the world's mythology: heroes and villains, fairy godmothers and wicked stepmothers, princesses and pig-keepers, prisoners and rescuers; ordeals and temptations, the quest for the magical object, the set of tasks to be accomplished. And a whole arsenal of cognominal swords, enchanted weapons; a wardrobe of cloaks of invisibility, seven-league boots; a whole zoo of dragons, helpful animals, birds, and fish. (172)*

Personal experience is a necessary, but not a sufficient, condition for writers to fully develop their craft. Writing that grows only from personal experience limits children and keeps them from using a source that the larger community of writers has historically drawn upon. According to Rosen (1982), narrative nurtures the writing process in that "we are always in a high state of readiness to transform into story not only what we experience directly but also what we hear and read." As I discovered during this study, child writers appeared to know this intuitively since they continually turned to literature and their past literary experiences while composing.

Classroom writing programs, then, should not be based solely on either personal experience or literary experience; instead, both should be used and numerous opportunities provided for writing and reflecting on writing. In answer to the question "Can writing be taught?" Barth (1985) appropriately responds:

> *Boyoboy, can it ever... authors have acquired their authority in four main ways—first, by paying a certain sort of attention to the experience of life as well as merely undergoing it; second, by paying a certain sort of attention to the works of their great and less great predecessors in the medium of written language, as well as merely reading them; third, by practicing that medium themselves, usually a lot... and fourth, by offering their apprentice work for discussion and criticism by one or*

several of their impassioned peers or by some more experienced hand or by both. (36)

3. *Children's literature is a source of authentic experience for child writers.* It could be argued that because literature involves vicarious (or secondary) experience, writing that evolves from it is inferior and contrived when compared to personal (primary) experience. Indeed, in terms of a sense of physical place, literature is a secondary experience. Whether they are reading or writing about Lewis's "Chronicles of Narnia" series, children experience the land of Narnia vicariously.

When the creation of language in order to "shape" another world through story is the intent, however, then interacting with literature, whether through reading or writing, becomes a primary experience. Experiencing literature directly involves child writers in the "spectator" role (Britton 1970). Through reading and writing literature in the spectator role, the children in this study were attending to writing for its potential to re-create past experiences and entertain future ones.

A basic psycholinguistic principle of learning to read is that children must be able to relate their prior knowledge to new experience (Smith 1971). This principle has also been applied to spelling (Zutell 1978), since children learn to spell as they compare their own attempts to spell a word with its correct spelling. Similarly, the literature of professional writers provides child writers with well-crafted models of how language can be used and shaped. The child writers in this study compared how professional writers used and shaped language to their own attempts to do so. This was especially evident as children returned to books during the writing process.

4. *The literature-writing connection is closely linked to children's intentions.* In addition to providing organizational structures that allow children numerous and varied opportunities to interact with children's literature, the teacher's role should be one of observing or "kid-watching" (Goodman 1978) and understanding children's intentions. This role is very similar to Smith's (1973) "one difficult rule for making reading easy," which is to "respond to what the child is trying to do." Observing and attempting to understand children's intentions enables a teacher to make informed judgments about what to say and do in the classroom.

The fact that children's intentions are context-dependent is precisely why literary links to writing can never become literary laws. If teachers are to become more aware of the literature–writing connection, they must learn to trust their own observations in the day-to-day classroom context. This recommendation is unlikely to be heeded by teachers or encouraged

Teachers need to respond to children in ways that enable them to explore options, make choices, and participate in meaning-making experiences.

by administrators, however, until they begin to reconceptualize the nature of teaching, learning, and the curriculum in a manner that acknowledges the dynamic nature of intentionality and context.

REFERENCES

Alexander, L. 1971. "High Fantasy and Heroic Romance." *Horn Book* 47: 577–84.

Barth, J. 1985. "Writing: Can It Be Taught?" *New York Times Book Review.* June 16:1, 36–37.

Britton, J. 1970. *Language and Learning.* Middlesex, England: Penguin Books.

Cooper, T. 1985. "A Note from the Editor." *Horticulture* 63:2.

Eco, U. 1984. "How I Wrote the 'Name of the Rose.'" *New York Times Book Review.* October 14: 1, 35–37.

Goodman, Y. 1978. "Kid Watching: An Alternative Strategy to Testing." *National Elementary School Principal* 57: 41–45.

Harvard Lampoon. 1971. *Bored of the Rings.* New York: New American Library, 1971.

Rosen, H. 1982. *The Nature of Narrative.* Paper presented at the annual meeting of the International Reading Association, Chicago. March.

Smith, F. 1971. *Understanding Reading.* New York: Holt, Rinehart & Winston.

———, ed. 1973. *Psycholinguistics and Reading.* New York: Holt, Rinehart & Winston.

Tolkien, J. R. R. 1965. *Tree and Leaf.* Boston: Houghton Mifflin.

Yolen, J. 1981. *Touch Magic: Fantasy, Faerie and Folklore in the Literature of Childhood.* New York: Philomel.

Zutell, J. 1978. "Some Psycholinguistic Perspectives on Children's Spelling." *Language Arts* 55: 844–50.

6

Excuse Me, Where's Your Teacher?

DONNA CARRARA

The crisp air of fall hit me as I walked out of the library of Teachers College, Columbia University. My thoughts, which had been focused on discourse in the classroom, turned quickly to steaming soup. Soup is always a panacea for facing that first hint of approaching winter. I look on fall as an interlude to prepare for winter, and like the squirrel that gathers nuts, I make soup.

As I walked into my house the phone was ringing. When I picked it up, a young voice greeted me on the other end.

"Mrs. Carrara, this is Robbie. I'm having trouble with a story I'm writing. I can't think of an ending. Will you have a conference with me?"

Robbie had been in my fourth-grade class two years before. He loved to read and write. It was always a pleasure to talk to him about the book he was reading or his current piece of writing. I eagerly told him I would be delighted to confer with him. In fact I was honored that he called me.

Since we live in the same town we settled on his coming to my home the next afternoon.

Robbie arrived with pens, pencils, books, and writing paper. A feeling of déja vu overwhelmed me as I looked at him. Although he had grown and obviously changed, I felt as though I was seeing an old friend again. I invited him to sit down at my dining-room table and tell me the focus of his assignment.

Robbie had to write a piece about ancient Egypt from the perspective of someone living in that culture. He had decided to write his piece as a nobleman. I asked him to read what he had written so far. Ancient Egypt came alive for me as I heard the culture and its people reflected through the story of a noble faced with the problem of people's refusal to pay taxes. When Robbie finished reading he looked up at me and said, "That's as far as I've gotten. I can't end my story."

"Robbie, remember when we had writing workshop in our classroom and I used to confer with you?"

"Yeah."

"Remember how I used to say that if you introduce a conflict in your story, you generally have that conflict solved by the end of your story. Well, the problem you need to resolve is that people are not paying taxes. Have you thought about your options?"

He didn't say a word. We were silent for a while.

"You know Robbie, while you put that idea on the back burner, do you mind if I ask about some other things I was curious about in your piece?"

"Sure."

As I asked questions piqued by what Robbie had written, my memory of what I had learned and read about ancient Egypt took on a new dimension. Through his narrative I had learned things that I wasn't aware of. As Robbie read the piece over, he also began to realize that he had more questions and needed more information. He started revising as he read, furiously jotting all over his paper. When he finished reading he announced that he was going back to the library to get more books. "Could I come back for another conference?"

"Absolutely!"

The doorbell rang the next afternoon and there stood Robbie once again ready to write. He told me that when he had gone home he had thought about some of the things we talked about, and that night he had made some changes. He wanted to read those to me and had brought several books he thought might be helpful. As he read one book I started to read another. I became hooked on reading about scribes.

"Robbie, I didn't know that scribes lived within a noble's estate."

Robbie looked up from his reading. "Yeah and...." In the next few moments I learned all about the role of the scribe.

When he finished, I asked him, "Why didn't you include that information in your piece?"

"I don't know, but I think I will, and I think I know where I can put it. I'm going to write it right now."

Robbie continued to meet with me until his piece was finished to his satisfaction. During this time we read together and wrote together (while Robbie wrote his piece, I listed questions that might help him as a reader and writer). We also discussed the qualities of good writing. I think Zinsser (1980) would be amazed that we pored over his book and that some of his cardinal rules of good writing helped Robbie. Robbie loved to use description in his writing, but he was guilty of clutter. Sometimes he would get so caught up with description that he would forget what he was writing about. Reading Zinsser on clutter helped Robbie to trim the description and maintain his story line. Robbie also took to heart Zinsser's advice on the importance of the lead. He played around with language until he felt the words he used would pull his reader in. He decided on dialogue for his lead and was very pleased with the way it sounded:

> *"I beg your pardon! My best census taker and you cannot do one thing about the people in the houses not paying tax. Forty percent of the taxes come from the people. What will Akhenuten say?"*

We looked at the conflicts Robbie had introduced in his story and at possible resolutions for them. This was most difficult for Robbie. He did not like to end his stories, nor did he like to edit. I asked him, "How would you like to read a book in which the author didn't give solutions to the problems he introduced?" He didn't say anything. That was Robbie's style. He would mull over anything you said and see how it fit into what he knew. Not receiving a response, I persisted, "Imagine in *Julie of the Wolves* [George 1972] if you didn't know if Miyax made it to civilization."

Finally he responded, "I wouldn't've liked it." This was a turning point for Robbie. He was finally able to think about concluding his Egyptian piece. In subsequent writing it became obvious that he had come to realize he could not leave his reader hanging, and it was easier for him to think about resolving conflicts.

The Effect of Research on Practice

Working with Robbie in a workshop atmosphere brought back many memories of my teaching experiences and the children I taught and learned with. I thought about how Lucy Calkins and Donald Graves describe the importance of establishing a workshop atmosphere in which writing and a community of learners evolve through a serious regard for the craft of writing (Calkins 1986; Graves 1983). Research on writing has had a tremendous impact on classroom practice. For me personally it was an impetus for the learning environment I was trying to establish. It complemented the literate classroom that was evolving as I learned more about reading and writing as a process and language arts as a dynamic state. My learning did not take place in a vacuum. I have had the good fortune to have a collaborative network with Dorothy Strickland from Teacher's College, Columbia University; Angela Jaggar and Bernice Cullinan from New York University; and Nick Aversa, a fellow teacher. Together we explored the relationship of reading, writing, and classroom discourse. Reading the work of researchers like Shirley Brice Heath (1983) and Judith Newman (1985) and journals like *Language Arts* and *The Reading Teacher* and being a participant in the Coalition Conference have influenced the way I view language arts in the classroom. I have come to the realization that it is not writing or establishing a writing workshop in and of itself that helps a child's literacy development. It is the reading, writing, and talking that take place in a mutual learning situation in which the teacher as well as the student is a learner. It is a closing of the distance between yourself and the students and assuming an inquiring stance. It is becoming a community of learners.

Within the classroom community, both the teacher and the children are active learners.

Robbie's visit brought about a myriad of reflections on what I have come to understand about the learning community. It also brought new understanding. A learning community is like a neighborhood. In a neighborhood people live and interact with each other based on their perceptions of neighborliness. Friendships are cemented through mutual care and respect for property and people. When the balance of the neighborhood is upset by a family moving away, new relationships develop. But when the family that has moved comes back to visit the old neighborhood, relationships are resumed as if nothing has changed. Neighbors know each other in a special way. Robbie's visit has led me to believe that the learning community is like the neighborhood. The residents of the community move on to another grade, but the bonds that are formed remain.

You all know each other in a special way. You have laughed and cried over a good piece of writing, a good book, or a conversation, and that makes the passing of time irrelevant. Members of a learning community can meet at another time, in another place, and pick up where they left off.

I can't reminisce without thinking about how it all began eight years ago. I teach in a school where learning is valued, where teachers participate in making curriculum decisions. Our curriculum is a framework adapted from the work of Morton Botel and JoAnn Tuttle Seaver (1977). The framework incorporates the following principles:

1. Children will read pieces of literature and respond to their reading in a variety of ways.
2. Sustained silent reading will be a part of every day.
3. Writing will take place daily in a writing workshop format.
4. The investigation of language patterns will take place in context.

When we implemented a literature-based curriculum the school principal realized that we were departing from the traditional basal format for reading and would need support. In-service workshops were given by the leading experts in reading and writing. People such as Dorothy Strickland, Donald Graves, Mary Ellen Giaccobbe, Nancie Atwell, Don Holdaway, and Toby Fulwiler came to speak to us. Mary Ellen Giaccobbe makes an annual visit. Her expertise as a first-grade teacher and a writer has been invaluable to our language arts program. Money was also made available so that we could continue our own education and learn more about what we later came to understand as whole language. We were encouraged to read, write, question, hypothesize, and sometimes fall flat on our faces. We were given ownership of and responsibility for our own learning. We were also given time to explore. We read, joined professional organizations, listened to one another, questioned, and probed for answers to the problems facing us every day. As teachers we became a community of learners.

All of this happened several years before Robbie, his classmates, and I came together to form our new community. Although I brought an understanding of children and language arts to the classroom that year, as every year, I am constantly learning more and seeing things differently. Annie Dillard (1974, 17) says "It's all a matter of keeping my eyes open," and that's what I've learned to do—keep my eyes and my mind open.

Reading Workshop

Robbie and his classmates remain vividly etched in my memory. That year was the year reading workshop was introduced. Don Holdaway had inspired several of us at a workshop we attended. I realized that the vitality I had as a teacher came through ownership of what happened in my classroom. I wanted the children to experience that vitality too. I felt that the more ownership and responsibility they had for their own learning, the more motivation they would have to learn. We already had writing workshop; now we would have reading workshop. In reading workshop, the children would self-select a book and read, and I would confer with them and keep a running record of the reading behaviors I observed (Clay 1983). The children each kept an individual reading log modeled after the log in Don Holdaway's book *Independence in Reading* (1980). When they finished a book, they knew a "response to literature" activity was expected. Such a response could be written (e.g., a play); it could be an artistic rendering (e.g., a setting collage), or it could be a dramatization, but it had to depict something from the book.

Just as in writing workshop, we spent considerable time in reading workshop establishing a routine. We began with a sustained silent reading time, which lasted about ten minutes. During that time we were all engaged in reading. I read children's literature as well as adult literature. After the ten minutes were up, a busy noise would start to permeate the classroom. Some readers would get up and move to the art table to work on projects, some would continue reading, and some would write in their journals about something in their story. We kept learning logs, which became dialogue journals I responded to. They were used in reading workshop and in other disciplines. If the kids noted something as they were reading that was significant for them, or if they needed clarification on a point, they understood that the learning log was the place to put it. Sometimes I would ask questions in the logs and the kids would respond. When we read *Tuck Everlasting* (Babbitt 1975), Janna, mulling over the idea of living forever, wrote in her log:

> *Beyond where the eye can see there is another world. A world where people never die. No one person is sure why. But many theories have come about us. I hide out from the light because I do live eternally. I can only wish that I didn't drink from the fountain when I was 20 be-*

*cause I still look 20. But I'm really 118. I drank from it
with all my friends, one cold summer night. I drank it to
show off how brave I was. But now I feel like a coward.*

When we studied the Woodland Indians in social studies, we read *Sign of the Beaver* (Speare 1983) and researched the Lenni Lenape Indians in depth. When a hypothetical problem was posed (Imagine that you are an Indian facing the white man coming and taking your land. How would you react?), Jeff wrote in his log:

*(From the Indian's Point of View)
White man. White man,
from over the sea,
go back to your homeland,
do not bother me.*

The conferences I had with an individual child often became group conferences. We all worked at understanding the plot, characters, and setting of a book. Personal evaluation of a book was considered equal in importance to any literal or inferential interpretation. It was a pleasurable time too. Friends gathered around a book to share their insights. The reader of the book held court, and often the questions asked by peers brought another level of understanding to the reader. The group conferences also had another effect. A book being discussed often became the hot book to read.

My role in all this was multifaceted. The time spent conferring about a book might become a time where I needed to intervene. If a book was too difficult, I would direct the reader to another that was more suitable, or I would challenge the reader if a book was too easy. I looked upon the reading workshop as a time to practice the skill of reading. Frank Smith (1978) says that readers need time to practice reading in order to become more proficient, and this was our practice time. It was a time during which different genres could be introduced. Most of all it was a time to talk with each reader and discover together what that reader needed to become more proficient.

I found myself examining what I do as a reader and reading about the strategies proficient readers engage in. Prediction and confirmation of predictions became a part of every workshop. What do you think will happen next? What made you think that? I looked at the cues the reader was using as suggested in *Reading, Writing, and Caring* (Cochrane et al. 1984). Did the reader use graphophonic, syntactic, and semantic cuing systems? What background knowledge did the reader bring to a particular book? If the background knowledge was sparse, was there somebody in the class who could provide information? Danny and Austin showed how important knowing about something can be to successful reading. Austin had suggested that Danny read *Song of the Trees* (Taylor 1975). Daniel was struggling through reading it and was about to give up when he asked Austin how he could read this book when it was so hard. Austin said, "Daniel, it's not a hard book. The language is different. You have to change the language in your head and then you can read it." The book was written in a southern dialect, and we had talked about how authors sometimes use regional dialects to make their books authentic. Austin had taken this to heart and shared his insight with Daniel. He then showed Daniel how to change the language. He read to Daniel, and as he read, he converted the southern dialect into standard English. Daniel said he would try to do that and continued to read. He did finish the book, and it was one of his favorites that year. Austin supported Daniel as a learner (Vygotsky 1962) and helped him find a way to negotiate meaning (Wells 1986).

The readers who had finished a book would go to the back table where art materials were available to work on a project that told something about their book. On the back wall was a list of possible projects we had brainstormed together. This list was a reference source if ideas were needed and grew as the year progressed. Some of the projects that might appear on the list were:

- Collage—character or setting collage.
- Story line—plotting the events of a story in sequence.
- TV script.
- Drama—turn a part of the story into a play and get some people to help act it out.
- Puppet show/script.
- Story map—a look at the story in terms of plot, characters, and setting.

The list began in September, and as ideas burgeoned it grew. Students were encouraged to come up with their own response ideas. When Annie read *Harriet the Spy* (Fitzhugh 1964) we were studying graphs and coordinates in math. As a response activity, Annie made a graph of the important events in the story with illustrations next to each point. In order to know what the points meant, the reader had to determine the coordinates and then look at another sheet that explained what incident the coordinates referred to. This response was more ingenious than anything I could have come up with. It exemplified the transfer of knowledge that kids can make if they are given ownership of their learning and respect for what they can do. Annie shared her idea with her classmates and helped anyone who was interested in making a graph. She gathered a few people around her at the back table and explained how she brainstormed all of the important events in the story before making her graph. She told them, "Use your math book to help set up the graph correctly." For Annie, reading and writing were important tools for discovering what you knew.

After reading *Tarantulas on the Brain* (Singer 1982) Jessica decided to make a game board. She wrote down the important events of the story and sequenced them in game form. Players moved forward and backward according to the event they landed on. A disastrous event could mean going back to the beginning. The rolling of dice and the movement of tarantulas spurred others to create a game board for their stories. Because Jessica had made miniature tarantulas to be used as pawns, the important characters of many a story became game pawns. The conversations and the collaborative nature of the art table inspired new ways of responding and continuously brought students back to their books for rereading.

The workshop always ended with a "pair share." We would gather around the room in pairs and for about three minutes we would take turns reading a part of the story we particularly liked, telling something new we had learned, or talking about a particular part of the story or a character. Sometimes I would go from pair to pair and listen to the children's sharing; at other times I would have a partner and share a part of my own book.

When I introduced the reading workshop, I started off by devoting only a small amount of time to it. I decided to increase the time in small increments. But I found that this period was so loved by the students that, as far as they were concerned, an hour a day was never enough.

The format was flexible. It was possible for a reader to be listening to a book on a tape recorder at the media center, reading with a partner if two people were sharing the same book, or sharing the reading with me. Courtney could not sustain a long period of reading unless she got up and read a part of her story to someone. Sharing brought her particular delight and helped her to verbalize her understanding as she read. The social context for learning (Vygotsky 1962) was important to all of us. The workshop was also a time when talking, writing, art, and drama were integral to reading.

Reading/Writing to Learn

Another part of the day was spent reading a whole class book. Multiple copies of the book were made available to all. During this time we would not only read but look at how the author used writing. The question became, "What can we learn from this author about writing?" When we read Roald Dahl's *Fantastic Mr. Fox* (1970) alliteration became the order of the day. We wrote alliterative names (Joshua Lite became "Lightbulb Lite") and alliterative stories, and the language experience chart filled up with alliterative poems. When we read *Abel's Island* (Steig 1976) we explored simile and metaphor. Thinking about this newfound device, Shannon wrote in writing workshop:

> **The Jungle**
> *I was entering the damp cool jungle, deeper and deeper I ventured. Slithering vines caught me tying me in knots strangling me until they let loose. I ventured even farther. As I was walking it started to rain, a tropical storm. It rained harder and harder! But I still ventured even farther. Bushes brushed against my legs making them feel prickly. Snakes slithered around me leaving a slimy yucky feeling. The light warm rain hit me washing the slime away. The strong wind blew my hair in my face making it all in knots getting caught on trees and vines.*
>
> *It was getting sunny and the rain stopped. I was out of the jungle alive!!*
> *"Shan, how did you like the car wash?"*

We read *Dragon, Dragon* (Gardner 1975). Poetry appears throughout, and so we studied poetry as a form. Luke wrote:

> *There once was a dragon so bad.*
> *It ate every lassie and lad.*
> *Till its head was beheaded*
> *The thing it most dreaded*
> *But the whole kingdom was glad.*

To explore how an author used a particular literary device or a pattern of language I would focus on it in context and then model something similar on the language experience chart. Modeling and giving students the opportunity to explore helped us all understand the various ways authors use language. We began to read differently. We read with an author's eye. After discussion and modeling I extended understanding by designing an activity. Students' response to the literature activity enabled me to see what, as readers, they understood about the story. The students who had a surface level of understanding were asked, "What made you think that?" When I could understand the thinking behind their response I was better able to help them reach another level of understanding. I designed the activity by asking myself one central question: "What would the learner learn from doing this?" I didn't want empty activities. An example: letter writing was the way Beverly Cleary wrote *Dear Mr. Henshaw* (1983). To explore letter writing I put the letter format on the language experience chart. As an activity, the kids would write and address letters. Jessica chose to write to Leigh Botts, the main character in *Dear Mr. Henshaw*. She addressed her envelope:

Leigh Botts
of the Little Cottage
With a 2 story
duplex in front
California

Her letter read:

127 Westview R.D.
Upper Montclair, N.J.
Jan. 9, 1987

Dear Leigh,
I understand how you feel about your dad. I think maybe you should try to keep your mind on something else. It would be hard but it's worth a try.
- *You could keep your lunch close to you to keep it safe.*
- *I am working on times tables in school. I'm improving.*
- *To make a friend: be nice to someone and they'll be nice to you. If you're lucky you will make friends with whoever is stealing your lunch. That way you will not have lunch problems.*
- *Leigh, Life is hard for you, but don't worry, you'll live through it.*
- *Do you like to draw? I pretty much do. You can create a whole new world on paper.*

Yours Truly,
Jessica Bruder

All of us, in some way or other, were deeply involved in promoting the use of literature in teaching children to read, write, speak, and listen.

The learning environment established in our reading/writing/talking classroom was one of collaboration. I was a collaborative partner in the learning process. So often I would hear someone say as she walked into our classroom, "Excuse me, where's your teacher?" I was one of the learners in the classroom, indistinguishable from the others. This delighted me because if I was truly engaged in collaborative learning with the kids, my presence shouldn't overwhelm the classroom.

In the kind of classroom I envision, the teacher is not standing in front of the room transmitting her knowledge to passive individuals. We—teacher and students—are all active participants. We are all at different points on a continuum of literacy development, trying to make sense of the barrage of information that surrounds all learners. We are all trying to make sense of who we are and how our understanding of the world fits into the fabric of the society we live in.

REFERENCES

Babbitt, Natalie. [1975] 1985. *Tuck Everlasting*. New York: Farrar, Strauss & Giroux.

Botel, Morton, and JoAnn Seaver. 1977. *Literacy Plus*. Washington, D.C.: Curriculum Development Association.

Calkins, Lucy McCormick. 1986. *The Art of Teaching Writing*. Portsmouth, N.H.: Heinemann.

Clay, Marie M. [1979] 1983. *The Early Detection of Reading Difficulties*. Portsmouth, N.H.: Heinemann.

Cleary, Beverly. 1983. *Dear Mr. Henshaw*. New York: William Morrow.

Cochrane, Orin, Donna Cochrane, Sharen Scalena and Ethel Buchanan. 1984. *Reading, Writing and Caring*. Winnipeg, Canada: Whole Language Consultants Ltd.

Dahl, Roald. [1970] 1982. *Fantastic Mr. Fox*. New York: Knopf, Bantam Skylark Book.

Dillard, Annie. 1974. *Pilgrim at Tinker Creek*. New York: Harper & Row.

Fitzhugh, Louise. 1964. *Harriet the Spy*. New York: Dell.

Gardner, John. 1975. *Dragon Dragon and Other Tales*. New York: Knopf, Bantam Skylark Book.

George, Jean Craighead. 1972. *Julie of the Wolves*. New York: Harper & Row.

Graves, Donald H. 1983. *Writing: Teachers & Children at Work*. Portsmouth, N.H.: Heinemann.

Heath, Shirley Brice. 1983. *Ways With Words*. New York: Cambridge University Press.

Holdaway, Don. 1980. *Independence in Reading*. Portsmouth, N.H.: Heinemann.
Newman, Judith, M., ed. 1985. *Whole Language: Theory in Use*. Portsmouth, N.H.: Heinemann.
Singer, Marilyn. 1982. *Tarantulas on the Brain*. New York: Harper & Row.
Smith, Frank. 1978. *Reading Without Nonsense*. New York: Teachers College Press.
Speare, Elizabeth George. 1983. *The Sign of the Beaver*. New York: Dell.
Steig, William. 1976. *Abel's Island*. New York: Farrar, Strauss & Giroux.
Taylor, Mildred D. [1975] 1978. *Song of the Trees*. New York: Dial.
Wells, Gordon. 1986. *The Meaning Makers*. Portsmouth, N.H.: Heinemann.
Vygotsky, L. S. 1962. *Thought and Language*. Cambridge, Mass.: MIT Press.
Zinsser, William. 1980. *On Writing Well*. New York: Harper & Row.

7

Constructing a Mosaic in the Context of Cultural Diversity

MARY M. KITAGAWA

"What are some of the things you have been wondering about?" I asked my class. Since I felt that the context of my question was clearly Outer Space, our current thematic unit, I was startled by the first response: "I have been wondering what it is like to have blue eyes."

Most years I am the only member of our classroom community who could answer that question. My sixth graders are nearly evenly divided between those who are Mexican American and those who are Native American (mostly Yaqui), with an occasional Vietnamese, Afro-American, or Anglo child. And also, since I sometimes identify myself with my husband's Japanese ethnicity, I almost forget that I have those blue eyes.

In a key statement, the Coalition Conference declared that "acknowledging diversity is the foundation of democracy. Responding to diversity is the foundation of a democratic education." This central concern intensified because 1987 was also the year a book that seemed to promote Eurocentricity (Hirsch, *Cultural Literacy*) became a best-seller, and English-only referenda were proposed in some states.

The metaphor of America as a melting pot fails to describe the diversity that conferees recognized as a vital dynamic in this country. A more appropriate image is that suggested by Shirley Brice Heath when she spoke at the conference. She introduced the metaphor of a mosaic: diversity that retains unique qualities while forming a pattern or scene. The elements of this mosaic include the diversity of all immigrants back to those who were on this continent first, the Native Americans.

Ethnic Identities Within the Mosaic

My Mexican American students can no longer give a tribal name to their Mexican Indian roots, but they seem to share with the Yaqui students a strong sense of identity with ancestral Indian and modern Mexican cultures. That sense of heritage might account for the difference I noticed in their approach to consecutive thematic units on the Middle Ages in Europe and pre-Columbian Mexico. Although they responded enthusiastically to doing research and preparing a mock medieval feast when we studied the European Middle Ages, they approached the content as they might read fairy tales or fantasy. When we moved from that unit into the study of pre-Columbian Mexico, however, they found it more like delving into a familiar folk tale.

Children's ways of knowing and learning reflect changes in society, in family, and in technology.

During the medieval unit the students leaned heavily on resource books to transform our classroom into the great hall of a castle. Their banners and paper "tapestry" decorations were closely copied from pictures in books. They were very knowledgeable after a month of study, but they could barely stay in character during the enactment of the medieval feast.

In contrast, we spent only seven days on pre-Columbian Mexico and the arrival of Cortez. Although we did not go into as much depth as in the earlier unit, students produced art and wrote without much consultation of published sources. They made a mural of the meeting of the Aztecs and the Spanish, composed their own "legends" about Quetzalcoatl, performed an improvisational drama, and danced as *viejitos*, "old ones," all with a minimum of rehearsal. As far as I can tell, this difference in comfort levels was not the result of previous academic study but rather of intuitive experience and identification.

I am convinced that it is only after recognizing their own cultures as acknowledged features of the national and world mosaics that students can become interested in the entire tableaux. This process requires real dialogue, real writing, and self-expressive opportunities in the fine arts. Because I want my students' understanding to reverberate from the familiar to the unfamiliar, I cannot rely upon prepackaged kits, textbooks, and commercially produced units of study.

Recently, a visitor to our school stood before some sixty students whose families, with the exception of one child from Vietnam, had immigrated from Mexico from one to ninety years ago. The visitor gave them his apparently canned spiel, "When you finish these activities you will realize that the culture of Mexico is not so different from our own." The children were too polite to point out the irony of his statement, but I was momentarily transported back to my earliest teaching days when I used the questions in textbook teachers' manuals. I was so eager to be in control that I sometimes skipped the questions in the teacher's manual that were followed by "Answers will vary"; I did not want to open floodgates I might not be able to close.

Through the years, under the strong influence of educators such as Kenneth and Yetta Goodman, Donald Graves, James Britton, and of Japanese teachers whom my husband and I studied a few years ago, I have come to realize that the only place real education *can* be grounded is in the "answers that vary." Open dialogue and expressive writing are a meeting ground for all of us as members of the classroom community.

Using Language to Contribute to the Mosaic

I ask students to write first for themselves. I put up a chart that lists a progression of responsibilities, the first of which is to draft and revise a piece of writing until it meets the writer's own expectations. Early in the year my students tend to hand me a draft of a piece and ask: "Is this good enough?" I have to turn the question back to them: "How does it meet the expectations you have as its author?" (I realized after a while that if I asked merely "Does it meet your expectations?" it was too easily answered with a simple "yes.") We talk about the feeling of satisfaction that washes over you when you read your own writing and know that it does accomplish your intentions. For many months, some continue to ask for my approval, but gradually most students come to appraise writing according to self-conceived purposes.

After attaining that feeling of satisfaction, students check with a trusted reader—classmate or teacher—for an audience reaction. The trusted reader is really a "listener" until the editing stage. I caution students not to show their trusted reader the page before editing begins, but rather to read it aloud so that mechanical errors will not be distracting. Editing comes last, and only after the writer and the trusted reader agree that the piece works self-expressively and communicatively.

It was under such guidelines that Rafael, for example, used writing to ease his sense of loss. At the same time he produced a touching memorial that made his audience appreciate "The Wonderful Dog I Lost":

> *I was at my mom's house and I remember getting my dog just before my birthday last year.*
>
> *My mom came home from the Humane Society with this little puppy. A day later I named him Sabbath.*
>
> *A week later my sister and I took him for a walk. He was so happy we decided to let him off the leash. He was chasing birds and playing in the grass; he was even wrestling with me.*
>
> *When we went home he fell asleep right away.*
>
> *My sister's cat, Chango, was smelling him and trying to get Sabbath to chase him. Then Sabbath woke up and barked at the cat, so the cat gave him a left hook right on the nose. You could hear the clap that the cat gave him. Sabbath started to chase him; you could hear barking and paws hitting each other. He went to my sister and sounded like he said, "Woof." My sister said, "Woof to you." Sabbath tilted his head and looked like he wondered, "You're a dog, too?" Sabbath got fed up and fell asleep again.*
>
> *About a month later I went back to my dad's house. He was washing dishes when we came in. He wiped his hands. When he saw the dog, he put the towel down and said, "Aw, Man," and he looked like he didn't want him. But the next day he fed him. Then he was petting him on the head.*
>
> *Just last month, Sabbath was huge; his paws went up over my shoulders when he stood up on his back legs.*

Constructing a Mosaic in the Context of Cultural Diversity

> *Three weeks ago he wandered off and he never came home. My mom and I went to look for him at the pound but we couldn't find him.*
>
> *On my birthday this year my sister Andi said to my brother and me, "Do you guys want a boxer if our dog has puppies?" So we said, "Yeah." She might give us two of them because one would be lonely.*

Rafael strained to capture every detail because he was preserving the memory of his lost pet. His commitment was more to Sabbath and to his own loss than it was to a readership. This is writing that served the writer first, and it happens to ring with Rafael's voice as a by-product of his need to write and of his personal perspective.

Rafael could also write impersonally with the same perseverence and sensitivity, as he did when he created his imaginary piece, "The Legend of Mount Saint Helens." His legend was about a goddess who was killed in trying to prevent the death of a deer. It ended:

> *About an hour later the ground started to tremble and the branches on the trees started to quiver. Then under her came a huge gigantic mountain. It lifted her all the way to the top and she disappeared but she left a ghostly swirl around the mountain. It swirled to the top and shot into the air and left a bright light in the sky.*
>
> *And to this day that mountain is still her. It is called Mount Saint Helens.*
>
> *Then everytime it erupts she is dreaming about the deer and the hunter, and when she gets to the part where she gets killed she lets out a big explosion and settles down again.*

Rafael "finished" this legend several times over a week of writing workshops. He was so in touch with his own inner voice that he continued to perfect it after his trusted readers expressed nothing but satisfaction. He had a stronger commitment to himself as a writer than to his peers as an audience.

Duyen's commitment was geared not to any readership but to her own understanding when she first wrote of her family's escape from Vietnam. She wrote about it so introspectively in her journal that the writing itself was disjointed. (She was free to use the journal for her own discovery because journals are not written for a general audience or to demonstrate writing prowess.)

Notice how Duyen alternated between her vague memories and her attempts to document the sources of her understanding:

> *When I was about 3–4 my mom and dad told my grandma that we were going to move to America. I was too young to know anything, so that's what I thought my mom and dad told my grandma.*
>
> *Tinh said that when I was 3–4 he was about 6–7 and he said that he would go to my grandma's house and eat the candy that she made in the morning, and go fishing in the afternoon with his friends.*

Her underlying quest for the picture of their life hung upon slim threads of memory and hearsay evidence. Duyen's story continued:

> *When we went we escapt on a small boat and when we [were] about in the middle of the ocean we meet a small boat, my dad told me all this when I was older, and when we did I thought that my mom and dad were leaving me so I cried. I think this was in my dream, but they were just helping me up to the big boat.*

And after another few paragraphs of speculative writing, Duyen ended with her theme, "I wish that I was older [then] so I could know more."

The journal seemed to serve Duyen as a springboard for further writing, a legitimate use of writing that is not available to students when writing topics and genre are strictly assigned. That year Duyen wrote often about Vietnam, basing her writing on interviews with her parents about their life there, the escape, and the grandmother left behind. In April she presented to the class a formal report about her family and culture. It included the comment "I imagine it was hard for my mom and dad to leave their family and home. Now I know what the price of my freedom is."

The next year her younger brother picked up the investigation but not in terms of the country he left behind at the age of two or three. Viet wrote about the Buddhist customs observed at home by his mother. About her prayer before an altar figure, he wrote: "You probably think of a little chubby man when I say Buddha, but I think there's two kinds of Buddha, that is, a chubby man and a lady Buddha." I asked Viet if he would interview his mother about these customs, but he chose to write only from his own observations.

Viet chose his topic after I presented to the class a series of three mini-lessons on extending single-event narratives to descriptions of their lives through some customary events. I used examples from former students' papers. The lessons encouraged, but did not assign, such writing. Joanna went on with her description of the rare occurrence of snow in Tucson; Rolando continued his monster fiction; and three students worked on written caricatures of their brothers, a kind of writing that was currently popular in a "Can you top this?" spirit. But Rolando was ready to describe his experiences as a Matachini dancer in the Yaqui cultural group of which he is a member.

In a poem earlier that fall, Rolando had included the line, "It [dancing] makes me feel like one of the elders." When he began to write this time about dancing in Yaqui ceremonies, he stated:

> *When I first started dancing at the Yaqui ceremonies, I danced at San Ignacio Church. And before I danced I had the butterflies. I almost ate a dozen tacos at my house because I was too excited. And then my cousin came for me because we were about to start dancing.*
>
> *The first song I danced I had been making everybody mix up because when the other people turned right I was turning left. That's because I was too nervous. After my third song I was okay....*

I joined him for a conference, following the content conference approach described by Lucy Calkins (1986). I wanted to know how he had learned the dances, assuming that training sessions had preceded his first public performance. When he told me that he learns the dances only by on-the-spot imitation, I was fascinated. I remembered hearing that Yaqui elders traditionally teach without explicit instruction, simply by including children in an activity. I hoped that my expression of intense interest would lead Rolando to add that information to his text. Though he seemed to enjoy my amazement, he chose not to include the information. From his insider's perspective this was not part of the story he was working out. He went on to describe the customs of farewell the dancers perform when a Matachini concludes his years of participation.

Rafael, Duyen, Viet, Rolando, and others wrote carefully out of loyalty to what they were documenting. Their classmates and I appreciated this because we too were striving for a faithful rendering of our experiences and ideas. This sort of writing community is not hard to build in a close-knit school in a small neighborhood that shares strong cultural bonds.

The Expansion of Consciousness to Include Larger Contexts

As sixth graders my students are fledglings perched for take-off because, for them, seventh grade includes a bus ride—to their first school experience as minorities in Anglo society. Some of them, if their older siblings' experiences are repeated, will suffer from taunting because of their ethnicity. As part of their preparation for entering into new relationships, we have become pen pals with sixth graders in a school of predominantly Anglo, middle- and upper-class students who will be their classmates in seventh grade. I was glad for the privacy of our classroom the day they received their pen pals' introductory letters. My students expressed their amazement with comments such as: "Listen to this! Listen to what she says about herself!" Some of their pen pals had presented themselves with a frankness that was not culturally familiar to my students: "I am one of the two most popular people in my class." "My mom drives a Buick." "I think I am pretty." Putting yourself forward in that way is not culturally appropriate to most of my students, but they will be schoolmates in seventh grade with students who do so under different cultural assumptions.

Another pen pal relationship introduces my students to middle school students from Shaker Heights, Ohio, including many who are their first black friends. These experiences help students like Rolando define their place in the national mosaic as they learn, for example, about rap groups from those who write their own raps.

In terms of cultural identity, these pen pal relationships are like stepping back from a mural to see how your part fits into the overall picture. Both of our sets of pen pal letters provide the correspondents at each end with between-the-lines texts about cross-cultural assumptions.

We also use literature as an avenue for seeing our cultures from other views. When they heard Omri, the main character in *The Indian in the Cupboard* (Banks 1980) expressing stereotypical views of Indians, my students exploded in anger against him and against the author. "What's that? You need a cowboy to play with an Indian!" they fumed, on hearing about Omri's assumption. Perhaps their reaction was intensified because just that week we had been on a camping trip in which we sat around an actual Hohokam pithouse site and imagined ourselves transported back into the days of those precowboy Native Americans. Sitting in a circle on a desert hilltop, we had imagined solutions to the daily problems of food, water, and shelter. We had watched as a teacher made tools from obsidian, built a fire by friction, and hurled a homemade spear, just as Native Americans had long before the first white cowboy set foot in Arizona. The students were not ready for even a British child like Omri to be so naive.

Later in the reading, they began to forgive the author when it seemed that her intention was to use Omri's ignorance and growing awareness to expose, not promote, stereotypes. The class discussed stereotypes associated with many cultural groups and played "catch the stereotypes" throughout the book, including some about cowboys. They were only ready to forgive the main character, however, when he changed his views. When Omri finally became open to learning about tribal distinctions from his small Iroquois friend and went to the library to get his information straight, Rafael sputtered, "Well, it's about time."

Some of the students also observed that Omri was more sickened by the image of Little Bear scalping French soldiers than scalping Algonquins. They could not decide whether to blame Omri or the author for such narrow-mindedness, but they were glad when Omri finally learned that scalping was an imported custom and not native to the Indians.

This sort of sharing of an interesting story while fretting over its ethnocentric caricatures may be valuable immunization for future textbook study. Most social studies books imply, as Omri does, that Indian societies are phenomena of the past. When one of my former students tried to point out that very failing in her high school American history textbook, her teacher accused her of having "an attitude problem." Her brother happens to be one of those in this class whose experience with *The Indian in the Cupboard* might help him with a rebuttal, should the same thing happen to him someday.

Curricular Decisions

Thinking is intertwined with language in a complex web of meaning that Vygotsky (1962) calls inner speech. The acts of expression that bring inner speech to the level of spoken or written words are not demonstrations of conclusions but processes that verbalize connections between experience and perception. When inner speech has no outlet in the classroom because talking and writing are merely recitation and performance, thinking becomes a performance instead of a tool.

Lately, in some curricular plans, thinking is being systematized under a capital T and made a subject with its own period of study. But isolating thinking as a skill to be practiced in exercises is like settling for a week of cultural awareness in an otherwise generic year-long curriculum plan. Neither will serve as more than gestures if the rest of the curriculum is steered by performance outcomes that are carefully predetermined by the teacher, a textbook, or a standardized test. We would never be omniscient enough to preprogram when children should write about a lost dog, an escape to freedom, a tribal ceremony, or a mother's worship habits. A required story starter would have complicated Rafael's construction of his Mount Saint Helens legend. Like thinking, writing occurs when need and opportunity meet. The teacher's contribution is the consistent scheduling of opportunities and the provision of a supportive milieu.

In my class we negotiate some curricular decisions even in content areas like social studies and science. It was not my blue eyes, but my graying hair that caused Gonzalo to wonder if we could study a song about Alexander the Great by his favorite heavy-metal rock group. He brought the tape because the lyrics dealt with that hero of the ancient Greek world, our current social studies topic. When we made it a lesson by listening to it and comparing the lyrics with information from an encyclopedia, I had to admit that the song was well-researched. Gonzalo and others gloated over having "educated" me and promised to be alert for rock music material we could use in our next unit, the Middle Ages.

After we brainstormed lists of what we knew and wanted to know about the Middle Ages, we discussed the format of our research. Although I heavily influenced the group decision to make a class book and end with a mock medieval feast, the students influenced me in return. They contributed many of the ideas for making the room look like part of a castle. Some students knew how to make "stained glass windows" out of tissue paper and black construction paper, so they taught the skill to others for our cathedral window.

I wanted to capitalize fully on the cooperative learning that these students seem to prefer to competition. Yet I wanted the cooperation to be built upon knowledge gained independently so that each student would contribute from a sense of expertise. I required that everyone read first on many subjects related to the Middle Ages. They could collaborate on reports, but I made a rule that no one could work with a partner until each had started a rough draft of a report on that topic.

I also wanted students to experience the malleability of texts that accompanies drafting and revising on a word processor, even though we had none in the classroom. I had to enter and then revise all versions of all texts using my own computer at home. Diane and Rafael were aghast when I suggested they combine their individual research papers about

> ...we have entered an era in which sociocultural factors figure prominently in the curriculum and practices of the elementary school.

armor, but they overcame their aversion to cross-gender pairing and collaborated well. Joanna and Cassandra understood the plague differently, but cooperated on a report titled "The Black Death." Leticia and Maria made charts and gave their report on heraldry orally so that our banners would have authentic symbols. Pancho used plastic blocks to make models of siege machines. His little siege tower had a working drawbridge; Eucario, who had written the most about sieges, gave Pancho advice about his model battering ram. Gonzalo read and wrote about Joan of Arc; Viet found more information and became Gonzalo's collaborator in revising his report.

Viet was one of the most popular collaborators, perhaps in recognition of his meticulous attention to detail. Adrian and Viet both wrote about falconry, but Adrian finished first. When the printout of Adrian's draft appeared in the working file, Viet joined him with his own handwritten draft. With scissors, glue, paper, and pencils, they combined information to make one report. They saved only two sentences of Adrian's original version, and very little of Viet's rough draft was incorporated without modification. They had to listen to each other intently to make the collaboration work. I heard them debating semantics and syntax; one argument was settled when Adrian compromised by ending a sentence with "a/the castle/s." They spread five resource books out, propping them open to critical pages for quick reference when information was the subject of negotiation. The draft shifted between them, sometimes even in midword, as each alternated with the other as writer or critic.

I was rewarded for being patient enough to update and reprint any number of new versions by the fact that the students would proofread meticulously and willingly rework a text they had thought finished the day before. Adrian and Viet, for example, were not at all concerned when, the day after their combined piece on falconry appeared, a classmate pointed out a sequencing inconsistency. They happily sent me home with more penciled changes.

In the end, our class book consisted of twenty-four reports, averaging about a page each of double-spaced typing. Thirteen were written by single authors, eight by a collaborative pair, and one by five writers; two were dictated to me by the entire class.

Whether friends are arguing over how to present the downfall of castles or reading a popular children's novel from multiple copies I have collected, the social nature of learning seems to be a critical element to my students. Cooperation is a commonly noted learning trait of Native American students, but I cannot prove that these students are not simply close because most of them have been classmates and playmates since preschool.

Our reading texts are trade books. The reading of some of them is simply an interaction of reader and text. But often friends choose to read copies of the same book, and I may be involved in the experience as a member of a literature study group. Sometimes I initiate the study, as when we moved from the Medieval Europe unit into the reading of three of the Prydain Chronicles by Lloyd Alexander (1964, 1965, 1966).

Instead of having students ask each other questions to check on reading comprehension, I try to steer the conversation to the connections we make between the text and our own lives or opinions. For example, whenever I am involved with a group reading *Tuck Everlasting* (Babbitt [1975] 1985), I have to find out who would or would not drink water of immortality as did a family in the story. The question has always started a lively discussion, and students quickly take over. In the story, the water locks you permanently into the age you are when you drink it. Although I always want to talk about the question of drinking or rejecting the water, every group of sixth graders so far has turned the discussion into a debate over the ideal age at which to drink it. I have begun to wonder if I am the only abstainer because I have already passed all the ages they say they would choose!

These reading groupings are built around students' interest in a book or their willingness to trust my judgment that they will be interested if they read a few trial chapters. As a consequence, students sometimes read above or below their "reading level" just as adults do. One of the positions taken at the Coalition Conference that pleased me the most was the recognition of the negative effects of early stratification and of tracking. We acknowledged that tracking may be rooted in our tradition of ability grouping for reading in the elementary grades.

Pancho is an example of a student who was labeled early as a nonfluent reader. Yet his contribution to discussions is consistently insightful. He brings to the group his vast general knowledge and his ability to glean the underlying themes of texts, even those beyond his apparent reading ability. Pancho was way over his head in *Ralph S. Mouse* (Cleary 1982), so apparently he skipped quite a few chapters in order to complete the reading on schedule. He confidently read the last part of the book, inferring to understand what he had missed. When he came to the final discussion, he declared, "There was nothing interesting for me from page 76 to 123 so I'll just listen to the rest of you when you discuss that part." It was a face-saving survival strategy, but it enabled him to remain a member of the group. Also, Pancho is so popular as a friend that better readers often join in when he forms a literature study group on one of the books he can read with ease. If Pancho were assigned to a reading group according to his scores on a standardized, multiple-choice test, he would be a group of one, and no one would benefit from his unique contributions.

The "Hidden Curriculum"

Students whose parents left the educational system at an early age may be particularly susceptible to what Henry A. Giroux (1983) calls the "hidden curriculum," the messages that children receive from the way knowledge is shared and classroom experiences structured. Children learn effectively every minute of the day but not always what teachers think they are teaching. Sometimes what children are learning is passivity, or that it is cheating if you skip an unknown word in reading instead of stopping to look it up, or that the teacher or the preprogrammed package is making all the decisions.

Experience tells us that when students have had their decision making restricted, sometimes by teachers who have also had their decision making restricted, they are more likely to become disenchanted with schooling. There are programs of instruction, for example, that purport to teach reading comprehension even though the accompanying hidden curriculum undermines the autonomy that reading requires.

Such was our experience with a computer software program once imposed on my students and me. It was a course of study that amounted to a computerized workbook, sans graphics, contextual wholeness, or real self-evaluation. My sixth graders were introduced by the software company representative to a data machine that spews out prescriptions on the basis of pretesting: "Do you see this box? It knows all about you: your name, your student number, how well you read, what you need to do to read better, and even what color eyes you have." The woman had to admit that she lied about that last point, but I wondered if it was just a slip of the tongue, since this program was being placed primarily in schools with the most minority students. In any case, the data box resembled the Orwellian Big Brother of *1984*.

The message to the students, then, was that their cooperation on these computerized tasks would result in reading proficiency. Later, they could take home a printout listing their mastery of such aspects of language as context cues and base words to reassure their parents as well.

What the students actually learned was that 85 percent accuracy was essential if they did not want to have to endure a repetition of a boring lesson. Their willingness to take risks hinged on a running mental tabulation of the number they had missed. (Maybe that is why, at the end of the year, the only real gain they showed was in math instead of reading.) When students suspected that there was danger of falling below 85 percent, they would desperately begin to con classmates and nearby adults into supplying a guaranteed answer. Students felt helpless in the face of ambiguous exercises and the arbitrary cutoff between success and failure. "What if it's wrong? I already missed another one."

The hidden curriculum was teaching students, especially the ones who most needed confidence, more about what they lacked than about what they could gain through diligent study. Here is an excerpt from a log I kept during the period in which we had to use these computerized workbooks:

> *November 25.... There was a paragraph (called a "story" although there was no real plot development) that described Cindy reading magazines in a waiting room. "Cindy's mother's big operation should be over by this time, Cindy thought. She wondered when the doctor would come out to talk to her." On this fragment of evidence, Kay needed to determine "the main idea of the story." She easily ruled out one of the three choices but hesitated between choosing "(A) waiting and worrying" or "(B) Cindy's mother's big operation." Kay told me, "Well, she was in a waiting room of a doctor's office, no, a hospital, because her mother was getting an operation." I knew then that she had read the paragraph successfully. But she still couldn't answer the question. Kay said she thought it was B, because having an operation was certainly more important than waiting for it to be over. She was unwilling to risk pressing the B key, however, without my confirmation. I was torn between wanting her to follow up on her own logic and knowing that she was going to get it wrong and have to repeat the whole lesson.*

Kay is one of the low-achieving students for whom this program was supposed to be the panacea. Unfortunately what she was learning was that she could not trust her own values when faced with school tasks. Thankfully, after a trial period, we were able to stop subjecting students to this program.

Commercial publishers can provide useful materials and suggestions for activities, but they cannot develop a learner-centered program for an individual school. A learner-centered language arts program must be created within particular communities of teachers and students.

Trust

A final dimension of seeing student diversity as a mosaic is the matter of trust. Inflexible curricular programs, such as the computer software described above, make implicit demands for one-way trust on the part of students. This is why the software company promoted the omniscience of the data box to the students. In the same fashion, the omniscience of textbook scope and sequence charts is presented to teachers as if there were concrete evidence to lock education into that schedule. Such demands for one-way trust make a mockery of the learning community that develops when teachers and students are mutually engaged in constructing knowledge from all available resources. In contrast to demands for unquestioning maze running by students, effective literacy learning occurs when students are trusted to want to read and write. The need to hear and produce stories is a common feature of all cultures. All that schools have to provide are consistent opportunities to meet that need and ways of refining the strategies children use in the reading and writing processes.

Reading and writing are powerful tools that enrich the context of anyone's life. Both are creative processes that enhance and celebrate the diversity of our populations. Well-written literature from one cultural group is inviting to other cultural groups because it speaks to the human experience itself. If the hidden messages that accompany reading and writing opportunities support students in interaction with their expanding world, these students can be trusted to become literate. As Frank Smith says, students want to join the literacy club partly because membership "adds to the individual's sense of personal identity" (1986, 38). From the viewpoint of personal identity, cultural identity, national identity, and a sense of history, all students should see themselves as vital to the overall mosaic of humanity. And that, it seems to me, is what education is all about.

Trust means valuing the learner as a human being who has much to give, demonstrate, and teach others. A trusted individual becomes a risk-taker, and to engage in learning is to engage in risk.

There is a strong fellowship of teachers who share the responsibility for mosaic-making by celebrating the human potential of students from all the diverse populations of this country. They are constantly ready to be informed by their students and never expect to be finished with that learning. They question prepackaged materials, decision making based on narrow, standardized tests, and powerlessness as a means of discipline. I would like to be considered a member of that fellowship of teachers.

REFERENCES

Alexander, Lloyd. 1964. *The Book of Three*. New York: Holt, Rinehart & Winston.

———. 1965. *The Black Cauldron*. New York: Holt, Rinehart & Winston.

———. 1966. *The Castle of Llyr*. New York: Holt, Rinehart & Winston.

Babbitt, Natalie. [1975] 1985. *Tuck Everlasting*. New York: Farrar, Strauss & Giroux.

Banks, Lynne Reid. 1980. *The Indian in the Cupboard*. New York: Avon.

Calkins, Lucy McCormick. 1986. *The Art of Teaching Writing*. Portsmouth, N.H.: Heinemann.

Cleary, Beverly. 1982. *Ralph S. Mouse*. New York: Dell.

Giroux, Henry A. 1983. *Theory and Resistance in Education*. South Hadley, Mass.: Bergin & Garvey.

Hirsch, E. D., Jr., 1987. *Cultural Literacy: What Every American Needs to Know*. Boston: Houghton Mifflin.

Smith, Frank. 1986. *Insult to Intelligence*. New York: Arbor House.

Vygotsky, L. S. 1962. *Thought and Language*. Cambridge, Mass.: MIT Press.

8

Encouraging Sixth-Grade Historians

DIANE T. ORCHARD

Our district's sixth-grade social studies curriculum includes a mandated nine-week unit of study about the state of Michigan. I generally begin that study by posing questions for the students to consider:

- Who were the earliest settlers in our state?
- When did they arrive?
- Where did they come from?
- Why did they come here?
- Where did they settle?

We first speculate on possible answers to these questions from general knowledge the children might already have. Next we verify our speculations by viewing films and reading excerpts from books about the history of our state.

As the students put together information from various sources, they quickly come to understand that the history of the state is composed of the somewhat parallel histories of individual communities. For instance, one hundred years ago an important Michigan industry was the logging of the great white pine, now the state tree. Students often have family stories about that era in our own community, since there were two large sawmills in operation here during the early 1800s.

This information sparks interest and inspires many questions from the students. Where were these sawmills located? Who worked at them? Where did the lumber go? How was it shipped? After discussion of the information in films, books, and personal stories, we list questions on the overhead we might want to answer about the history of our own community. We then make a "web" of the questions by grouping them in broad categories (see Figure 8–1).

Webbing, a brainstorming process akin to free association, is a useful method of developing curriculum because it helps students see relationships and make connections. While our curriculum grew well beyond the original web as the interests of the students expanded, initially students focused their research on the part of the web that was of particular interest to them.

After we decide what information is important to us as class members, we also brainstorm ideas for how we might gain this information and how we might like to present our findings and to what audience. This gives us a goal to aim toward and some sense of direction in our study. Each year the original web is different and the ways we seek information, and present that newfound information, take on different forms, adding additional resources for future reference. And even though we study the same general topic every year—the history of our state—each class, because of the unique strengths and interests of individual students within it, has added previously unearthed facts and interesting tidbits to our store of information. What is reinforcing for me, as a teacher who once felt constrained by the history textbook as a source of curriculum instead of as a resource, is that students in later years still have excitement in their voices as they remind me of what they learned about Michigan in the sixth grade.

Our hope is that when children leave the elementary school, they will be on their way to full participation as citizens in our democracy.

Encouraging Sixth-Grade Historians

Sample Beginning Web

Figure 8–1

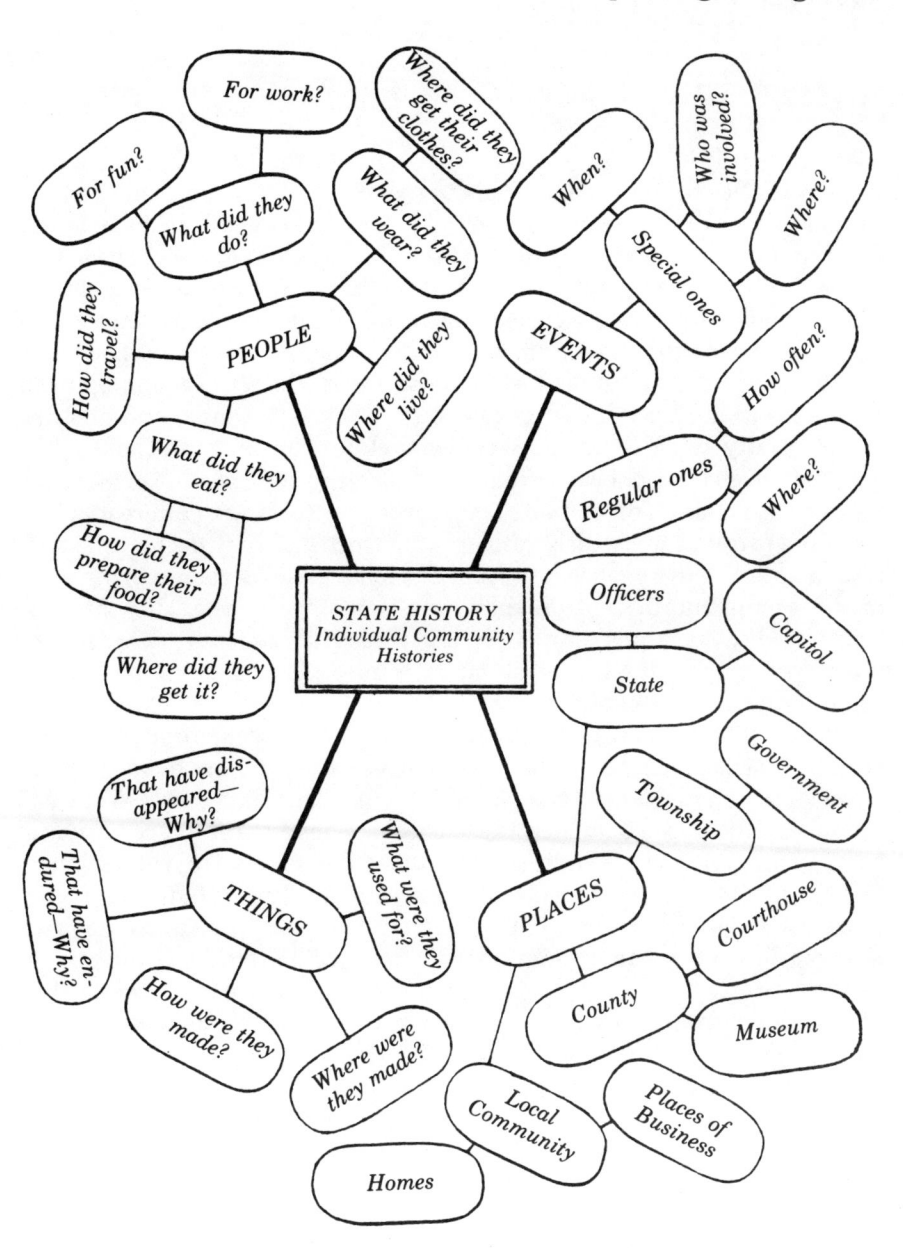

- STATE HISTORY / Individual Community Histories
  - PEOPLE
    - What did they do?
      - For work?
      - For fun?
    - How did they travel?
    - What did they wear?
      - Where did they get their clothes?
    - Where did they live?
    - What did they eat?
      - How did they prepare their food?
      - Where did they get it?
  - EVENTS
    - Special ones
      - When?
      - Who was involved?
      - Where?
    - Regular ones
      - How often?
      - Where?
  - PLACES
    - State
      - Officers
      - Capitol
      - Government
    - County
      - Township
      - Courthouse
      - Museum
    - Local Community
      - Places of Business
      - Homes
  - THINGS
    - That have disappeared—Why?
    - That have endured—Why?
    - What were they used for?
    - How were they made?
    - Where were they made?

The Research Process

Organizing Information

Each student keeps what we call a "journal"—actually a folder with end pockets inside the covers and brads to secure writing paper. On the first page of this journal the area of interest appears as a heading. I have found that having convenient repositories for different types of information can be helpful in assuring that important or interesting facts do not get lost. Our journals with pockets are especially useful for specific unit researching and information collecting, but writing folders, spiral notebooks, or simple tagboard-covered booklets may serve as well. It is also helpful to have a booklet especially for unfamiliar vocabulary words, and another one especially for dated notes on movies or classroom presentations.

After preparing their journals and selecting the area of greatest interest to them, students get into small groups according to interest areas. With the original web still visible on the overhead, they decide who will respond specifically to each question. Students are expected to bring back to the group information on their question(s). However, they are not limited to the questions they select, and if several students are especially interested in a particular question, they may each research it and pool the information they gather.

We may seek answers to questions like: What occupations were important in this community one hundred years ago? How have they developed and changed over the years? Why has this happened? What has influenced the speed at which these changes have taken place? Finding possible answers to these questions involves the use of all of the language arts: students *speak* and *listen* during personal and group interviews, class discussions, partner or teacher conferences, and class presentations; they *read* cemetery tombstones, maps, reference materials, letters, newspaper articles, books, government records, and anecdotal records; they *view* pictures from many sources, films, and videos; and they *write* notes, journal entries, letters, and articles.

Field Trips

One of the ways students find answers to their questions is by going places. When I suggested a visit to a cemetery and asked, "What kind of information might we be able to find there?" this was the response:

"Well, for one thing," Shannon said, "the headstones could be good sources of historical information...like, well...what were some frequently occurring family names in this community? They might have been important in its development."

"How many generations can we find in family plots?" Billy wondered.

"What was the most common boy's first name in the 1800s? or girl's name?" Kathy suggested.

"What names don't we hear any more?" Michele said.

And our history buff, Damon, added, "Who was born during the Civil War? or the Korean War? or Who served in two wars?"

"What good will this information do us?" I asked.

"Well, from this information we can decide which people we might want to get some more information about. Maybe we can tell who were influential families," George answered. "Some of those families may even be relatives of some of us!"

"Yeah. Can we take some measuring tapes along so we can find out who has the biggest headstones?" Brian asked. "And we could find the smallest headstone, and then we figure out what the average size was."

"...And ages....How old did most people live to be back then?..."

"Could we take some paper and crayons along in case some of us want to do some crayon rubbings of tombstone carvings, or sketch pretty ones?" asked Doris.

And so the cemetery proves to be a primary resource as we begin our study, and a rich source of notes to be recorded in our journals.

Our next visit is to the village offices to meet officials and learn the functions of local government. While there we read historical documents. We learn that the first formal meeting of local government in our community, as in many communities across the state, was held almost 150 years ago, in 1842. And we learn which families were active in the early days of our community, which ones were influential, and which ones are of interest to particular students.

We look at early maps of the area published in 1874, 1893, and 1906. The skills of map reading, such as determining directions and interpreting scales, begin to take on a purpose when we attempt to make sense of the early geography of our community.

"How come this lake is named Mud Lake on this map and Grass Lake on this other map?" Greg asked, noticing a discrepancy while comparing maps.

"Where was the first school located before it burned?" Lisa wanted to know after reading that the school burned in 1926.

And Frank asked, "How far apart were the two logging mills?" when

A curriculum area like language arts should be concerned both with what students need to know and with what they are able to do. Knowledge is part of being able to do, just as being able to do is part of knowledge.

he was looking at the registration forms of the local mills in the township books.

I make copies of some of these early maps for our later perusal and study. Some will go into student journals and some will become "class copies." There are also pictures of early landmarks, which I am granted permission to copy. The resources available for use in our classroom have continued to grow over the years. For instance, two older gentlemen of the community, during two different time periods, wrote their remembrances of life in our township during their lifetimes. On one of our trips to the local newspaper plant, I was able to make copies of their articles, which have now become available for reference in our classroom. I have also made copies of pictures from the village office, from newspaper articles, and from privately-owned photographs. These photos were made available to us by individuals in the community who have become aware of our ongoing interest. The photos are now part of a continually growing classroom photograph album. With each new class of students comes an additional source of pictures: "My grandma has a picture of the old mill...."

We then visit the county courthouse (the oldest in our state) and the county historical museum to see artifacts of earlier days. We look at atlases from the 1800s and a history book of our county, published in 1884. Those students who have chosen to research the use and/or production of "things" have a heydey here as do those who are researching special events, because there are many posters and political buttons on display in addition to the collection of artifacts and clothing.

Interviews with Resource People

We invite local senior citizens who have lived in our community all their lives to come into our classroom and tell us what they remember of their own childhood days as well as what they remember hearing from their parents about earlier days in this county. Before our guests arrive, the children and I generate questions we want to have answered, so that during the visit the students are all waiting to get the specific information they seek. Students discover that not only are interviews excellent sources of authentic information, they can be entertaining as well.

One visitor brought willow branches and showed us how to carve willow whistles, a popular, useful toy of his day. Another visitor showed us how to make a self-propelled vehicle, created with a wooden spool, a rubber band, and a toothpick. I have found that it takes many examples of a world without our modern conveniences for children of today's high tech society to gain any real understanding of the ingenuity required just to entertain oneself in a world without electricity.

I also encourage students to seek information through individual interviews, either in person or by letter. In their journals, they keep copies of the letters they have sent and received as well as their interview notes. They have had the interview procedure modeled for them in the group interviews we do in class, and we brainstorm ideas for other kinds of questions they might ask. We have developed a form that makes it easier for respondents. This form provides space for the date; the name of the person being interviewed and his or her relation to the interviewer, age, and place of birth; and sections for details of the interview. Students may use it during a personal interview or include it with an introductory letter.

We have received some most interesting anecdotes. One interviewee told of how her father built a car from scrap parts. It had no body, just a frame, floorboards, and a windshield. The children had to hang onto the back of the seat to keep from falling out, whereupon her father made "seat belts" to tie them in. She said she remembered doing everything in this car, and noted that it would not even be allowed on the road today.

Another interviewee told of a game played much like Hide and Go Seek. Children hid while two participants threw a ball three times over something quite high, yelling, "Roller, roller, three times over, if you don't holler, we won't foller." Then the two seekers called, "Whistle if you're near, holler if you're far, if you don't holler, we won't foller," as they tried to find the hiders.

Standard letter writing form becomes a necessary tool when students seek real information from real people. Clarity takes on new significance when students know they must assimilate, analyze, synthesize, and then share the pertinent information. Daily journal writing and note taking become important when students want to record "interesting stuff" so they won't forget it.

Sharing the Results

Students are continually sharing newfound information with each other—sometimes excitedly with the whole class, as when a letter arrives from an interviewee; sometimes in more formal small-group sessions; and sometimes just with individuals, as time and interest allow. At each juncture, additional facts are being added and meaning is being constructed in a unique way for each participant in the study. I help students establish some checkpoints along the way—times and dates by which they should have field notes complete or final drafts ready.

A final step in the learning process is presenting knowledge in the forms we selected at the start of our study. During the local history study described here we decided to produce a booklet of activities and to create and then produce a play for fellow students.

We worked on the booklet first, with each area's small group deciding how they would present their findings. We looked at many other publications for ideas. It was the large group's consensus that they wanted it to be a "doing" book, one that other students, brothers and sisters, or even moms and dads could have fun with. And so, participants in each group selected their own task(s) to complete. The results ranged from a board game and "match-ups" to mobiles and models of historical buildings to cut and paste. My role was that of encourager, advisor, editor, proofreader, and typesetter. Our local vocational-technical school students did the actual printing. The booklet ended up being twenty-six pages long and included a contribution by each student. We distributed copies to each contributor and then sold additional copies to recoup printing costs.

As soon as we had taken the booklet manuscript to the printers we began in earnest to put the play script together. Because of the talents and enthusiasm of class members this particular year, the play ended up being a more elaborate presentation than I had ever attempted with a class before. Some students who lived in town and could walk to school met me an hour before class each day, and several others stayed after school to help create the stage. We made the eight-foot stage in sections, which we then bolted together for the stage wings. Discarded red satin drapes made stage curtains, as well as covering the wings.

The nurturing classroom climate empowers all learners to seek meaning through reading, writing, listening, and talking and to be continually involved in active inquiry.

The children selected a "character" that particularly interested them from our community's past and created a three-foot tall stringed marionette to represent that person. And since every early logging camp had horses and dogs, we had two horse puppets and a dog as well. We constructed the puppets with assistance from parents, the principal, and the art teacher.

We wrote a script that included each character the children had selected. As they shared the information they had gleaned, it seemed to fall into three general categories. Act 1 focused on the logging camp. Several students were interested in how it had operated, where the workers came from, and how the logs were moved from the camp to their destination. Terms from the vocabulary books, such as "choppers," "swampers," and "skidders," became a part of this act. A second act seemed to focus on downtown Attica in the 1880s because so much information had been gathered about the local businessmen of that time and about the lumberjacks' interactions with them. The third general area, which became act 3, had to do with an influential businessman, Mr. Williams. He owned not only one of the two sawmills but also the major hotel at the time, Williams House. It was a popular bar and eatery for the townspeople as well as the lumberjacks.

I worked with small groups on dialogue, script form, and stage directions as we "walked through" the play informally. Some information from journal notes just had to be put into the play, like this entry from Greg's journal: "One time, at a downtown hotel, an inebriated logger danced on the wooden bar in his spiked logging boots and gouged out pieces of wood that onlookers described as being 'as big as toothpicks.'" Greg and his friends had to figure out how to make props that adequately expressed this occurrence to our audience.

Eventually, the thirty-three sixth graders created their three-act play from information they had sought out themselves, synthesized, and then presented in a new form, to a new audience. The local press and parents were invited to one of the performances, after which we served punch and cookies. We videotaped a performance to add to our classroom resource collection. That tape has now been used by several community groups for special programs.

During another year's study of our state's history, students chose to write letters to authors living in our state requesting information and a favorite recipe. As a final project, we produced a thirty-three page cookbook, containing biographical and historical data and the favorite recipe contributed by each author. The students and I also included our own favorite recipe and biographical information about ourselves as authentic, published authors in our own right. After providing each contributor with a complimentary copy, we sold additional copies of the cookbook to interested family and friends to help with printing costs. Several of these special recipe books, complete with laminated covers and plastic binders, are now in public libraries across our state.

In the culmination of yet another year's study, we cooperated with other teachers and students in our school to re-create a day in the life of a student in our community one hundred years ago. From various individuals' research and field notes we were able to supply participants with copybook specifications, authentic elocution lessons, songs and games of the period, and directions for making real turkey-feather quill pens and homemade blackberry ink. We all dressed for the period, and we even imported outdoor toilets for the day.

Throughout my teaching experience I have found that learning can be a joyful experience when both teacher and students are seekers of meaning in a supportive learning environment.

9

Reading, Writing, Rappin', and Rollin' Your Own

MARY MERCER KROGNESS

Lamont, his twelve classmates, and I had just finished reading James Clavell's *The Children's Story*, a symbolic novel about a classroom of seven-year-olds, vulnerable because of their youth. The children, except for the skeptic, Johnny, are taken over in just twenty-five minutes by New Teacher, who is a foreigner, an infiltrator, and a member of a totalitarian government. My kids were noticeably intrigued with this story, at first because it was short and the print large; later because the terror of it piqued their curiosity. We hashed over the tactics New Teacher uses to accomplish the takeover. Together we uncovered other big issues in the work: the importance of time in a novel, vulnerability, characters' motives and reactions, disregard for the individual and individuality. We also discussed the fallacies of rote learning, since the seven-year-old students in *The Children's Story* say the pledge of allegiance, by rote, every day in school. But when questioned by New Teacher (who recently has arrived on the scene) about what the words *pledge* and *allegiance* mean, the seven-year-olds retreat, overwhelmed by their ignorance.

Fourteen-year-old Lamont is a member of my first-period eighth-grade language arts/reading class designed especially for kids who are below the local fourth stanine in reading, who have elected not to take a foreign language, or who have washed out of the foreign language program. When I asked my students to respond in writing to whichever part of the story touched, interested, or puzzled them, Lamont decided to write about the dangers of rote learning. While Lamont was in the process of writing in his notebook, I walked by his desk to confer with him briefly. Lamont pointed to his piece and asked, "Is this the way you spell *rote learning*?" Curiously, he'd spelled *rote* "remote." Remote learning! A symbolic error, indeed. I suspect that Lamont as well as Greer, Brandon, Madelynne, Alphonso, Kenya, Jason, Leshawn, Renaldo, Latrice, Benita, Marlon, and David have for many years been engaged in various forms of "remote learning" experiences because early on, these young people, all minority students, had not successfully mastered the intricacies of reading; their modes of learning often differed from the mainstream white and black students in the Shaker Heights, Ohio, schools. Many of my students had not had the benefit of early language making and using (i.e., being read to as young children, being talked with during the formative years, being exposed to a variety of rich experiences, including imaginative play) that encourages talking.

The Fallacies of "Remote Learning"

Because Lamont and others like him weren't yet able and perceptive readers, writers, and thinkers, and because many were or became behavior problems, I suspected from watching and listening to them that they had been fed a pretty steady diet of highly structured and didactic worksheets designed to inculcate isolated reading skills, worksheets that denied them, however, the essence of language-rich literature. They had been given writing assignments, usually book reports, in which a premium was placed on the technical aspects of writing but not on the promise of creating one's own stories, poems, plays, songs, slogans, speeches, and letters. The "remote learning" that Lamont referred to in his response to literature heightened my awareness of the effects of programmed learning on my students: reliance on prescription, acceptance of homogenized materials such as basal readers, comfort with intellectual drudgery. Because such materials are shallow, they don't have the power to engage students actively and quicken their imaginations. Neither can a language landscape, replete with imagery, nor a love of literature be developed when young people are spoon-fed. This sort of desolate academic experience precludes a meeting of mind and spirit in the classroom. It rules out talking.

Filling out worksheets, putting them in a bin labeled *Finished*, then working their way through a big box of color-coded cards containing bland and artificial stories that are accompanied by sets of questions, all foster dependence. During one class period, when we were engaged in doing improvisational drama, Kenya blurted: "All we do in here is sit around and talk, do improv, and write. When are we going to get down to *real* work? My mother wants to know." I questioned what she meant. "I mean doing real hard work like book reports and worksheets. What we do in here is fun, Mrs. Krogness, but...."

In my zeal to involve Kenya and her eighth-grade classmates actively in listening, talking, reading, and writing—imploring them to take responsibility for their own language learning—I realized that many of my students didn't understand the significance of these kinds of offerings. The educational value of fashioning an ordinary bandanna into a newspaper, then a checkerboard, or a banana being peeled, or of using the scarf to play the role of a bull-fighting matador, eluded most of them—even though they were visibly pleased when I praised them for these, their own imaginative responses.

Many of my students saw drama not as a tool for using language imaginatively or a means of impromptu thinking and talking but as a way to have fun in class. Examining a tea bag and letting it spur their thinking and remind them of, for example, a clock's pendulum, a parachute for Stuart Little, a book bag for a mouse, a box kite flown by a grasshopper (all ideas they concocted in class) made them wonder what my purpose was for engaging them in such playful activity. When I explained that using the imagination and creating images were important to thinking and using language richly, many looked perplexed.

We collected a variety of contemporary black expressions for a dictionary. My eighth graders looked incredulous when I explained that such an activity was valid because it made obvious the nature of language: that is, language is created by ordinary people like us rather than linguists and dictionary makers; language constantly evolves and changes as it is used and must do so if it is to remain vibrant. The facts, the straight facts, seemed more important to many of my students. Kenya and many of her classmates couldn't fathom the importance of sitting around the conference table talking and raising questions about the personal stories they

...without the space, the time, and the materials for dramatic expression and play, the child cannot rehearse the adult he or she will become.

were in the throes of writing. Kenya verbalized her concern that playwriting in a reading and language arts class seemed silly.

Small Signs of a Learning Community

My seventh graders, who are more even emotionally and malleable than the eighth graders, grew comfortable with being members of a community of learners who regularly talked, wrote, and read. Many remained at the conference table long after they'd heard our suggestions about the writing they were working on, long after they had responded to questions posed by their classmates and me about ways to sharpen the focus, develop story characters, or use language more imaginatively. But learning quietly, and often in isolation, had been and often still was customary for them and therefore comfortable. Our classroom was noisy. Frequently it was too noisy for a few students to work. But most of the seventh graders appeared to accept—even flourish—in this free-style operation in which students were expected to talk and ask more questions than the teacher and make decisions about using time. They adapted to these ways more readily than, for instance, my first-period class of thirteen eighth graders, whose mercurial ways contributed to my intermittent uneasiness about the language learning that was taking place in Room 226 or the student-centered classroom I was still struggling to establish with them.

Initially, the eighth graders were delighted with the offerings: they were regular recipients of elaborate letters from me about their writing and about themselves as writers. They read my letters eagerly. Generally they were pleased to engage in lighthearted, apparently undemanding activities such as playing theater games. Less often, they were willing to attempt discussing issues in literature and life as well as writing personal stories. Many, however, flourished when they gave speeches about themselves. They held up family photos, biking gear, car models, and other memorabilia while they talked. Speakers played favorite tapes. Jarrett, who aspires to be a professional basketball player, talked about his dreams while dribbling a basketball across the classroom floor instead of relying on notes written on three-by-five cards. Small groups of students used their voices and bodies to perform Maya Angelou's poem "Harlem Hopscotch," wrote and performed ingenious raps in response to Eve Merriam's poem "I'm Sorry Says the Machine." We taped Virgil while he belted out this original response to Merriam's poem about the mechanized, detached world we live in:

Virgil's Rap
This is information—
What city, please?
I said, Heaven,"
She said she could get that with ease.
Then she came back and said,
"Temporarily out of order."
So I dug into my pocket and pulled out another quarter.
She said, "Dial one."
And that was the end.
So I hung up the phone and tried my call again.
The last four digits ended with seven,
"You have reached the res-i-dence of Heaven."
I didn't know what was up,
But I knew it was wack,
"If you leave your name and number
We'll call you right back."
At the tone of the beep
It came to my head—
I cleared my throat
And this is what I said:
"I'm Virgil B. and I'm from Earth, you see.
You can call me at 921–3593! Rap!"

After we had read and chanted Bobbi Katz's poem, "Samuel," about a child's finding a salamander "near a pond in the woods" and taking the little creature home and then to school where it "died very quietly during spelling," Devon wrote a stunning poem. Katz's clean, unpretentious language, the cadence, and the reflection on childhood touched something in Devon, who wrote about a personal experience. Here is Devon's free-verse poem, "Jesus He Was, Jesus With the Eyes."

I went to Grandma's funeral
and saw a picture of Jesus.
    Jesus he was,
    Jesus with the eyes.
Right away I ran to Mom
and told her of the sight.
    Jesus he was,
    Jesus with the eyes.
I looked at the picture, up and down.
I looked at it 'round and 'round

> *to see how real he was.*
> *I walked two steps up*
> *and two steps back—*
> *No matter, he was*
> *Jesus with the eyes.*
> *Sometimes I wonder if he was in the picture.*
> *(Is there really a Jesus? I don't know.)*
> *Sometimes I wonder.*
> > *Jesus he is,*
> > *Jesus with the eyes.*

But some grew restive. They forced my hand by being unresponsive, even sullen and uncooperative. A few dared to act out (not dramatically, either) and yell irrelevant comments that derailed us. When they were in this mood, they collaborated, not to stir each other's thinking, but to make chaos. The community that I had my heart set on developing with my students (and heretofore had managed to do for twenty or so years) wasn't taking shape.

Colleagues whose opinions I respected advised me to tighten my control. They suggested assigning seats rather than letting students sit where they wished, giving homework and tests, writing detention referrals, putting those who disrupted the class repeatedly out of the room immediately and letting those who vacillated between being passive learners and obstreperous disrupters—occasionally ubiquitous classroom characters—know that I was in charge. Let those students know with certainty that here was the seat of authority. I was the old dog being taught new tricks. But some of the tricks I considered learning were not compatible with my philosophy or even vaguely similar to the old and freer methods of teaching I'd used successfully for many years to build, with my students, a classroom climate that was conducive to conversing and exchanging ideas or, as Kenya put it, a classroom where "all we do is just sit around and talk."

The challenge to lead all of my students beyond what they already knew, engage them in ways in which they'd possibly never been engaged before, and free them to take charge of their learning and indeed their lives, was before me. I was sustained by empathic and enlightened colleagues who valued engaging learning experiences that asked—demanded—the students' personal investment; I was renewed by highly prized moments such as that euphoric day when we launched a discussion, apropos reading Clavell's *The Children's Story*, about oppression and liberation in our own lives. Greer, a bright boy whose eyes burn like hot coals when he speaks, talked passionately about being black and what it

---

...we resist the notion that either the perceived problems of the children or of the teaching situation provide ready-made excuses to give in or to give up.

means to be black in a society that doesn't value him. Madelynne's voice rose as she told about her mother's struggle to become a nurse while she raised a family and held down a job. I fantasized that my first-period class, all of whom talked openly that Friday, would internalize the promise of this bright and shining moment; that this coming together through words would stir in them a desire and need to test their ideas. But on the following Monday, several students sashayed into class late while others sat glumly. When I asked Latrice to spit out her gum, she slouched in her chair and then aimed the pink wad toward the wastebasket at the front of the room.

For so many years I'd been open to my students' ideas, often seizing upon their desires and basing activities—even whole units of study—on their interests. Several years ago, my sixth-grade students and I were deeply immersed in studying the Renaissance. An art historian visited our class to talk about Renaissance painting and sculpture. After she finished showing slides of the frescoes Giotto had created by painting on wet plaster, Stephanie wondered aloud: "Why can't we make a fresco? If fresco-making means painting on wet plaster, why can't we paint on that wall of our classroom that is wet and always peeling?" Although we didn't paint a fresco on the wet west wall of our classroom, we did take Stephanie's suggestion. With the help of a Cleveland artist who specialized in restoring frescoes for the Cleveland Museum of Art, twenty-five students and I designed and painted two forty-four-by-forty-inch frescoes on canvases of plaster.

The Importance of Talking

Learners who are members of a community bring ideas to the group. They play active roles and take responsibility for responding, thus becoming invested contributors. Some members who are reticent must, in Brandon's words, "be lifted up." But even reticent community members learn to enjoy the rewards that come from active participation. By responding—by initiating—a student, by definition, takes responsibility for her or his own learning as well as for the learning of others. The joint effort can be pleasing and energizing to community members because collaboration implies active participation; yet it also precludes the individual's assuming the full burden. Each person has the opportunity to be stimulated by the ideas and insights of others and gains immeasurably from a free exchange.

While I watched and listened intently to my students, I realized who was assuming most of the responsibility for the learning, who was trying to create an atmosphere in which we could work peacefully if not vigorously. It was I. I brought to class and read aloud young adult literature that often was not well received. I endeavored to engage my students in discussion about issues related to both literature and their lives, only to face indifference, a consequence of their history. I implored them to begin viewing themselves as learners, only to be told by their eyes and attitudes that they were content to leave learning to others. Some of my students had failed too often and for too long. But I had forgotten the small but significant bits of growth: Fredrick, a learning disabled student who all but refused to join in most class activities, gave a stunning speech about himself while he held up various props that prompted his thinking. All eyes were riveted on him. Brandon, a bright boy who was retained in seventh grade and who exhibited impulsive behavior, thrived on writing personal stories and receiving daily letters from me about his writing. Brandon, for a time, helped me to corral his classmates. Tomika, alternately petulant and articulate, initiated a meeting with our assistant principal, who came to our fourth-period class to talk about the separation of black and white students during lunch and socials, a topic of great interest. Talking was becoming central to my classroom. Talking during class and after was important. I frequently telephoned both students and parents in the evening to explain what I wanted to accomplish; to express pleasure to them about specific pieces of work or unusual class participation; to set limits for behavior within a classroom setting. All of this talking allowed me to inform, to teach. My own talks with many colleagues, my principal, and two assistant principals—all available, informed, receptive, and also desirous of finding better ways to tap our students' potential—buoyed me as well as gave me, too, a sense of community.

How difficult it was to know the effects of our coming together and charting new courses. Donald Murray once said about writing that the most important part of the word *revision* is *vision*. Feeling as though I were the lone architect of my classroom, perpetually in a quandary and in a constant state of revision, I decided to sit back, gain a little distance from the day-to-day skirmishes, and look at the big picture. I lacked perspective and vision. Which students were developing a feeling for language and making progress as language learners? The majority, I estimated. This realization persuaded me to rule out adopting the empty vessel theory—merely filling up all those heads with fare that could be directly administered and easily quantified. I held fast to the belief that the whole-language, student-centered classroom was the only classroom

---

When a child has opportunities to choose materials, work in a variety of situations, and interact with all class members in an environment that is predictable but not static, exciting but not chaotic, and disciplined without being restrictive, the child is more likely to become a responsible and responsive member of a learning community.

worth designing. During this time of regrouping, I recalled the words of ethnographer and anthropologist Shirley Brice Heath: "The *back* in back to basics is oral language." Talking—the basis of communicating and learning and coming together. I would continue to make talking the focus. Talking is, after all, the heart of the matter; it is also a matter of the heart.

But for my first-period students I would have to set tighter limits, provide a routine and therefore a more reliable structure within which we could work. Systematically and patiently I would try to ignite my most passive or cautious students while looking for ways to channel the often ill-spent energy of those who most frequently acted out.

Creating a Climate for Learning

Creating a climate, an atmosphere for language learning, that is free but not permissive, exciting yet not chaotic, disciplined without being restrictive, a classroom in which a lively exchange can take place, is an enormous challenge. This was especially true in terms of still other important variables that lay outside my control. Although the majority of my students were, from my observation, of average—even above average—intelligence, they were often labeled basic students. These young people often traveled together from class to class all day. Thus, they enjoyed no respite from each other. New members and new combinations of learners brought little freshness to their school experience. Basic classes of between ten and fifteen students, designed especially to provide an optimum learning environment for untraditional learners and underachievers that was manageable in size and scope, were luxuriously small. But these students were sentenced to live and learn with each other daily. Stoking their cerebral fires, therefore, was a formidable challenge. The insular nature of this learning environment, while in many ways secure, was not usually conducive to fresh and vigorous thinking. For lack of a better term, intellectual and social incest often resulted. (The positive and negative effects of tracking students are constantly being weighed and challenged by teachers, administrators, and parents in our school district. I, too, am struggling to come to grips with this critical issue. Certainly, absolute answers are not forthcoming).

Time was another variable to be considered. Time, like ownership and response, was an essential ingredient for creating a classroom climate in which give and take contributed mightily to the freedom, vigor, spon-

Within a five-hour school day, extended blocks of time permit the teacher to weave the various aspects of the curriculum into a rich fabric.

taneity, and energy as well as to all language learning. In the elementary school from which I'd come, time, uninterrupted blocks of time, was like manna from heaven. Now, as a middle school teacher, I was hard pressed to capture imaginations, harness a considerable quantity of adolescent energy, enjoy with my students the luxury of going off on tangents, correlate language making with literature, play with words, bring the reading aloud of fine literature together with listening experiences and talk to our hearts' content when the class period was barely forty minutes long. The rhythm of a forty-minute period is stiff and syncopated, like a cha-cha, perhaps; an open-ended school day is fluid like a waltz.

While certain variables, such as the magic or machinations of adolescence, are in a state of flux, other factors, such as the tracking system and inflexible class schedules, are often fixtures at the secondary level. (At the Shaker Heights Middle School, however, a variety of possibilities for more flexible scheduling are being considered.) Acknowledging institutional limitations is important; being prime movers in changing those variables that can be changed is critical. But in the meantime, I am committed to finding ways of tapping the natural resources sitting before me, letting, in James Moffett's (1987) words, these young people speak in "active voices."

I dream of the day when I can haul into the classroom my collection of more than five hundred paperbacks—contemporary young adult novels—because I am certain that my students, at this juncture, can go it alone; can sustain interest and attention long enough to get hooked on Mildred Taylor, Lloyd Alexander, Katherine Paterson, Virginia Hamilton, Eve Merriam, Sue Ellen Bridgers, Myra Cohn Livingston, Cynthia Voigt, Langston Hughes, and others; can come to the conference table ready to talk and write about what they think and feel about books *they* have chosen to read. In the meantime, with many of my eighth graders I face new and heady challenges that haven't merely raised my anxiety level. They have filled me with new zeal and determination to trust my instincts and, with my students, to find ways of coming closer to achieving a classroom climate in which talking is central. In Peter Elbow's (1973) words, "A teacher has to learn how to roll her own." And I am doing just that.

REFERENCES

Angelou, Maya. 1971. *Just Give Me a Cool Drink of Water 'fore I Die*. New York: Random House.

Clavell, James. 1981. *The Children's Story*. New York: Dell.

Elbow, Peter. 1973. *Writing Without Teachers*. New York: Oxford University Press.
Heath, Shirley Brice. 1983. *Ways with Words: Language, Life, and Work in Communities and Classrooms*. Cambridge: Cambridge University Press.
Katz, Bobbi. 1973. *Upside Down and Inside Out*. New York: Franklin Watts.
Moffett, James. 1987. *Active Voices II: A Writer's Reader (Grades 7–9)*. Portsmouth, N.H.: Boynton/Cook.
Moffett, James, and Betty Jane Wagner. 1968. *Student-Centered Language Arts and Reading, K–13: A Handbook for Teachers*. Boston: Houghton Mifflin.
Murray, Donald M. 1976. "Revision: The Process and Strategies for Intervention." Rutgers Invitational Seminars on the Teaching of Composition.
———. 1982. *Learning by Teaching*. Portsmouth, N.H.: Boynton/Cook.

Epilogue
Memories to Grow On
JULIE M. JENSEN

As you read *Stories to Grow On* you heard the voices of eight of your contemporaries. Their goal was to transport you to their classrooms in a way that only a story can do. But each of us has our own stories to tell, and not all of those stories are set in the present. We were all students of the language arts before we were teachers, and our memories can be a powerful source of stories to grow on. I invite you to join me on a trip into the past where we will search our school years for models of teaching that inspire growth. As a storyteller, I hope you will invest your tales with detail as rich as your memory allows.

Here are some milestones in my life as a public school student in small-town Minnesota:

- The day we made butter, and the time we spent constructing, stocking, and staffing a grocery store in Miss McNelly's kindergarten classroom.

Epilogue

- The trip Miss Heidinger's fifth-grade class took to the state capitol building in St. Paul.
- The weeks in Miss Ardolf's sixth-grade class when we created a half-scale papier-mâché giraffe, which we donated to a Minneapolis children's hospital.
- The trial-and-error search with a classmate for the identity of a chemical element presented to us in Mr. Summerfield's senior chemistry class.

What I knew during those days and weeks of kindergarten, fifth grade, sixth grade, and twelfth grade was that school was immensely important to me and that I couldn't wait to get there. How could I miss a chance to churn, to say nothing of taste, our own butter? How could the class grocery store possibly open without the day's cash register operator? How could a giraffe get built without the assistant chair of the paste-mixing committee? How could I miss a close-up look at the gold horses at the base of the capitol dome? How could Georgine, my chemistry lab partner, identify zinc without me?

What I know now is that I had four teachers who could plan and guide not only memorable, but instructive, English language arts experiences. As butter makers we learned lessons in how to listen to each other and to adults, how to read a recipe, how to follow directions, how to take turns, how to report a school activity to those at home, and how to invite the school principal to an important event without forgetting essential information. As grocers we learned how to make cooperative business decisions, how to read and compose ads, how to label and price merchandise, how to fill out order forms, how to please a customer, and how to respond to a complaint. In order to go to the capitol we learned how to plan a trip—where to write and what to find out, how to listen to a tour guide, how to ask appropriate questions, how to record key information, and how to write a news story upon our return. (Unfortunately, my friend Janice did not learn how not to throw up on the bus.) As giraffe-makers we read about size, shape, and color, we became planning committee members, we developed a schedule, we composed letters to possible recipients, we arranged for delivery, we made an informative and gracious presentation, we were interviewed by the local newspaper, and we composed a photographic scrapbook of the stages in our process. As teenage chemists we learned the importance of collaboration, of reading detail, and of recording observations with precision and in a standard form.

I dredge up these details for anyone who needs reminding that making butter, running a successful grocery store, constructing a papier-mâché giraffe, taking a field trip, and identifying a chemical unknown are basic.

They are not "enrichment" experiences intended to occur after the "real" business of the school is conducted. They *are* the real business of the school. One cannot engage in experiences such as these without learning how to learn, without becoming a better listener, speaker, reader, and writer, to say nothing about learning lessons in social studies, science, and mathematics. Most obviously, one cannot be a participant in experiences such as these and be left without memories.

This book is a salute to teachers who touch the hearts of students, teachers who create communities of language learners where memories are built. It is also a forum for expressing concern. While I am sustained by exemplary teaching in many classrooms I visit, by the work of talented teachers I read about in the professional literature, and by my own good memories, I despair of the prominence of those who would have us teach facts, of those who think the answer is skills, of those who would respond with yet another test, of those who constrict, constrain, impose. And I must confess that, while some of my own school memories sustain me, more of them escape me. I did not confine my sharing of school experiences to five because of space limitations or because of compassion for you, my readers, but because the well ran dry. The memories I detailed for you were the exceptions.

My professional views today are influenced in no small measure by the nameless and faceless who never let a meaningful experience interfere with their dedication to the gnats' eyes of the teaching world. For me, as for many students today, school was for the most part an undifferentiated blur, a prolonged sequence of dispassionate, unconnected motions. With few exceptions it was neither engaging nor affecting, and it is not memorable. Skills were taught in the absence of any function apparent to us and without content of enduring value. Content was transmitted without a meaningful context and without our involvement. Preoccupation with the head was nearly complete.

Tuned-out students aren't new. Critics of the schools with simple solutions to educational problems aren't new. Forgettable teachers aren't new. Neither are teachers with large measures of practical wisdom new. But it is those teachers who *know* and *can do* who are more important as a source of insights for the improvement of teaching than we have acknowledged. Who can demonstrate better than they the range of talking, reading, and writing that can go on and for what purposes in an instructive and memorable language learning community?

Let me give you a few examples of what Miss McNelly, Miss Heidinger, Miss Ardolf, and Mr. Summerfield knew and could do.

They knew something about those buzzwords of the day—*ownership* and *empowerment*. Our talking and reading and writing were about *our* butter, *our* grocery store, *our* trip, *our* giraffe, *our* experiments. How significant that we thought *we* were in charge. Ken Macrorie likes to call our guiding hands "enablers," not teachers. Though these enablers never read Macrorie's book *20 Teachers* (1984), they certainly knew about drawing out learners and challenging them to produce good work. They got to know us; they created circumstances for our learning; they made it possible for us to succeed. We felt pride, and power, and confidence.

These teachers knew something about social learning as well as individual learning. In all the memories I shared, I was a member of a learning community rather than an individual in a captive audience. My teachers didn't seem to think that we would come to control our worlds through language if they held the view that all learning came from them. We interacted with each other as well as with the teacher; we talked, read, and wrote together in order to carry out personal and social goals that were worth achieving. Yet I doubt if any of these teachers consulted John Dewey (1916), Jerome Bruner (1971), or Margaret Donaldson (1978) on the power of social learning.

These teachers seemed to understand that every one of us came to school with ideas, interests, worries, and feelings of our own. We all knew about and cared about something. And, in all likelihood, that is exactly what we were eager to talk about, read about, write about. I know my teachers didn't read Neil Postman's (1979) views about personalizing language experiences for students, yet when we learned the format of a business letter we learned it in the context of a piece of discourse that was compelling to us; it was a form we needed to use in order to accomplish our purposes. When it was time to make written arrangements to visit the capitol in St. Paul, my teacher did no cajoling. She depended on no textbook or workbook, and we took no multiple-choice test on terms like "salutation" or on the placement of a comma in a date. Our agendas were fully compatible. How did she know without Postman to tell her that "language growth originates in the deepest need to express one's personality and knowledge, and to do so with variety, control, and precision"? How did she know that using language, knowing, and living are supposed to be intertwined?

These teachers knew the meaning of active learning. Instead of listening to a warmed-over lecture or completing an assigned textbook reading, we saw, tasted, touched, and smelled what we talked and read and wrote about. We visited a grocery store, walked the aisles, interviewed an employee—all of which stimulated more talking, reading, and writing. My teachers didn't read John Goodlad's *A Place Called School* (1984). No matter. The flat, unaffecting, passive classrooms he observed are not places they would understand. It wasn't for them that he wrote:

> *The relentless monotony of telling, questioning, textbooks, and workbooks which we found to be so characteristic of classes from the fourth grade up must be in part replaced by activities calling for student involvement in planning and in the collaborative execution of plans....In the process they read, write, compute and deal with the problems of people, their environment and the relationships among them....A major problem of schooling is the degree of unconnectedness it often has with reality beyond the school. The incongruity between school as it is and the lives they are living makes much of school meaningless. (335)*

To all of these teachers, language made no sense unless it was whole. Attention was directed to its significant use in integrated and worthwhile experiences. We didn't have to be told to be convinced that language had practical value in our lives. We seldom used language to talk about language; we used it to talk about our world. We began with things worth doing, then, moved by our interest, acquired the needed skills.

These teachers knew something about the raw materials of learning. They appear to have shared a view that it's difficult to be passionate about the contents of a textbook. We learned from talking to people, from examining and experimenting with materials in the classroom, and from going places, most particularly places where good books could be found. From a book about running a dairy, a book about Cass Gilbert, the architect of the state capitol building, and books about giraffes we learned the power and the promise of reading. My teachers would never have prompted Lynne Cheney to write about textbooks as she did in *American Memory* (1987), for they seemed to have a taste for materials that increased the appetite for reading and modeled fine writing. In general, they saw more instructional promise on a Wheaties box than in a teacher's manual. Though they were more likely to know Rachel Carson for her book *Silent Spring*, they seemed to subscribe to her philosophy of education expressed later in *The Sense of Wonder* (1956). In my favorite passage, Carson recounts the experiences she shared with her nephew Roger:

> *When Roger has visited me in Maine and we have walked in these woods I have made no conscious effort to name plants or animals nor to explain to him, but have just expressed my own pleasure in what we see, calling his attention to this or that but only as I would share*

discoveries with an older person. Later I have been amazed at the way names stick in his mind, for when I show color slides of my woods plants it is Roger who can identify them. "Oh that's what Rachel likes—that's bunchberry!" Or, "That's juniper but you can't eat those green berries—they are for the squirrels." I am sure no amount of drill would have implanted the names so firmly as just going through the woods in the spirit of two friends on an expedition of exciting discovery. (18)

Implied in all of these overlapping descriptions of my larger-than-life teachers is a call to dust off some age-old ideas about the role of meaning in the school experience. The best possible environments for language learning are not prepackaged through legislation; they are not ready-made between the covers of a textbook; and they are not revealed in published test scores. Growth is not installed from the outside for teachers or for students. Instead, it is active; it is personalized; it is collaborative. It is nourished by conversation, by reading, and by writing among teachers, administrators, parents, and students.

Just as students need to hear and see, talk and share, read and write in order for meaning to emerge from their experiences, so, too, do teachers. The best among us are not purveyors of facts and skills, not sages; they are learners. They are not teachers of *writing* and fonts of knowledge about the true meaning of a literary work, they are *writers* and *readers* who know how to guide other readers and writers in a supportive environment. For most of us, our task is to try less hard to be teachers and to try much harder to be learners—to teach as we were taught in the best of our memories.

All of us have Miss McNellys, Miss Heidingers, Miss Ardolfs, and Mr. Summerfields to take cues from and to express gratitude to. They showed us how to learn from experiences that interested us and involved us deeply, they celebrated our good work, they made us feel proud and accomplished, they preserved our curiosity, and, clearly, they built memories that endured. They enriched our minds by touching our hearts, and they did it in the most delightful, artful, and powerful of ways—through language.

REFERENCES

Bruner, Jerome S. 1971. "The Process of Education Revisited." *Phi Delta Kappan* 53: 18–21.

Carson, Rachel. 1956. *The Sense of Wonder*. New York: Harper & Row.
Cheney, Lynne V. 1987. *American Memory: A Report on the Humanities in the Nation's Public Schools*. Washington, D.C.: National Endowment for the Humanities.
Dewey, John. 1916. *Democracy and Education*. New York: Macmillan.
Donaldson, Margaret. 1978. *Children's Minds*. London: Fontana.
Goodlad, John. 1984. *A Place Called School*. New York: McGraw-Hill.
Macrorie, Ken. 1984. *20 Teachers*. New York: Oxford University Press.
Postman, Neil. 1979. *Teaching as a Conserving Activity*. New York: Dell.

*In the end education
is an act of faith in the power of ideas
to have consequences unforeseen
and unmeasurable.*
—*Neil Postman*
    Teaching as a Conserving Activity

The Authors

Carol S. Avery is a first-grade teacher at the Nathan C. Schaeffer Elementary School, Manheim Township School District, Lancaster, Pennsylvania. She is a teacher/consultant for the Pennsylvania Department of Education Writing Project, a founding member of the Children's Literature Council of Pennsylvania, and a member of the National Council of Teachers of English and the International Reading Association. An author of several articles on teaching children to write, she has also presented numerous teacher in-service workshops and spoken at professional conferences. She has taught at Eastern York High School and Millersville University. Presently working on an M.A. in writing at Northeastern University, Ms. Avery received a B.S. and M.Ed. from Millersville University.

Fredrick R. Burton is an elementary instructional specialist at the Upper Arlington public schools in Columbus, Ohio. A specialist in curriculum and instructional development, evaluation and qualitative research, and reading/language arts/elementary education, he holds Administrative Specialist and Elementary Principal certificates and was the recipient of the "Golden Apple Award" for Teacher of the Year in the Upper Arlington public schools. Dr. Burton is also a visiting professor at the University of Northern Michigan, has consulted at various schools in Ohio, and serves on the National Council of Teachers of English–sponsored National Committee to Evaluate Curriculum Guidelines and Competency Requirements. The coauthor of *Reading and Literature*, he has also written for ERIC and publications such as *Language Arts* and has spoken on the writing process of children, grading, textbooks, children's literature, and reading comprehension. He received his B.S., M.A., and Ph.D. from Ohio State University.

Donna Carrara is the grade level chairman at the Montclair Kimberly Academy in Upper Montclair, New Jersey, and recently taught a course at Teachers College, Columbia University with Dorothy Strickland on language arts and the elementary school child. She has published in *Language Arts*, is a reader of literacy proposals for the U.S. Department of Education's Office of Educational Research, and has piloted a new literature-based reading program that evolved into a whole language-based language arts curriculum. Ms. Carrara has spoken at or participated in numerous workshops sponsored by the New Jersey Association of Independent Schools, New York University, Montclair State College, Columbia University, the University of Pennsylvania, the International Reading Association, and the National Council of Teachers of English. She has also consulted for the *Encyclopedia Brittanica* and Disney Productions. She received a B.A. in education from William Patterson College, an M.S. in teaching and curriculum from Teachers College at Columbia University, and is currently working on an Ed.D., also from Teachers College.

C. Jane Hydrick is a second-grade teacher at MacArthur Elementary School, Mesa Unified School District, Mesa, Arizona. She is also a faculty associate for educational media and computers at Arizona State University. Ms. Hydrick is currently serving as the codirector of the seventh annual Microcomputers in Education Conference, the president of the Arizona Chapter of the International Interactive Communications Society, a member of the Elementary Steering Committee of the National Council of Teachers of English, a member of the NCTE Task Force on Teacher Competency, the elementary editor for the *Newsletter of the Assembly for Computers in English*, and a member of the Review Board of *Language Arts*. Ms. Hydrick is the editor of *Ethics and Excellence in Computer Education: Choice or Mandate?* and a contributing editor to the Apple Company's series of *Curriculum Guides for Software*. She was a Romper Room teacher for western states ABC affiliates from 1966 to 1969, and in 1985 she was named Tempe Woman of the Year. Ms. Hydrick received her B.A. from the University of Arizona at Tucson, her M.Ed. at Arizona State University at Tempe, and is presently studying there for her Ph.D. in communication arts/educational media and computers.

Julie M. Jensen is Professor of Curriculum and Instruction at The University of Texas at Austin. She was the 1987–88 President of the National Council of Teachers of English and has served as president of the Central Texas Council of Teachers of English, editor of *Language Arts* (1976–1983), and as a member of various committees for the Conference on English Education, the NCTE, and the National Conference on Research in English. Professor Jensen is the editor of *Composing and Comprehending* and is the coauthor of *Measures for Research and Evaluation in the English Language Arts*, Volumes I and II, and *Developing Children's Language*. In addition, she has published extensively on writing, teaching, and the profession for such journals as *Childhood Education, English Education, Journal of Reading Behavior, Research in the Teaching of English, Elementary School Journal,* and *Language Arts*. Professor Jensen earned her B.S. in elementary education, her M.A. in curriculum and instruction, and her Ph.D. in education at the University of Minnesota.

Mary M. Kitagawa teaches at Richey Elementary School in Tucson, Arizona. She has written on verbal humor, composition, and Japanese education for such periodicals as *Language Arts* and *The Reading Teacher* and for numerous Japanese publications. The winner of a special award from the Arizona English Teachers Association in 1982, Ms. Kitagawa has also taught in elementary schools in Michigan and Massachusetts. She received her B.A. in Education at the University of Massachusetts and her M.A. in English as a second language from the University of Arizona. She also participated in a seminar on language and learning at Theobald's College in England.

Mary Mercer Krogness has just finished a year of teaching English and language arts in the Department of Education at Cleveland State University as part of the Visiting Instructors Program. Previous to that she taught writing and language arts in the Shaker Heights City Schools in Ohio. Ms. Krogness wrote and produced "Tyger, Tyger, Burning Bright," a widely honored writing program for children on PBS. In addition, she has served as a member of the Elementary Section Steering Committee of the National Council of Teachers of English and a member of the Editorial Board of *Language Arts*, and she is currently a member of the

The Authors

NCTE's Task Force on Excellence and the Children's Literature Association Notable Books Committee. Ms. Krogness is the author of *Houghton Mifflin English*, a sixth-grade English text, and numerous articles on the teaching of writing and language arts. She received a B.A. in English and a B.S. in elementary education at Ohio State University and an M.A. in education at John Carroll University.

John C. Maxwell has been with the National Council of Teachers of English since 1971, serving as Executive Director since 1981. He has also been a teacher and administrator at a number of institutions, including the University of Illinois at Urbana-Champaign, the University of Minnesota, and the University of Wisconsin. Dr. Maxwell is the author of *Backgrounds in Language* and the coauthor of *Dialects and Dialect Learning*. In addition, he has published many articles on teaching and the profession. He earned his B.S. in education and his M.A. in English education at the University of Nebraska and his Ph.D. in educational policy studies at the University of Wisconsin.

Diane T. Orchard teaches at the Lapeer Community Schools in Lapeer, Michigan. She has taught grades 1 through 7 and 10 in public and private schools in Michigan, Kentucky, and Hong Kong. The author of articles in *The Michigan English Teacher* and *Resources in Education*, she has been a presenter at over thirty workshop sessions for local, statewide, and national conferences. In addition, she has contributed to the Michigan Department of Education's new publication on writing and illustrated three books of poetry. She received a B.A. from Asbury College, an M.A. from the University of Kentucky, and a Ph.D. from Michigan State University. Her dissertation was a descriptive study of a primary teacher inservice support system for writing instruction.

Susan Stires is a primary resource teacher for kindergarten through grade 3 at the Boothbay Elementary School, Boothbay Harbor, Maine. She has also taught learning disabled students, reviewed books for Heinemann Educational Books, and read innovative grant proposals and served as a member of the Language Arts Advisory Committee for the Maine State Assessment for the Department of Education and Cultural Services of Maine. Ms. Stires has done consulting work and presented papers in the fields of writing process, primary writers, and learning disabled writers for the National Council of Teachers of English and for a number of schools and institutions. She has written chapters for several books, including *Teaching All the Children to Write*, *Academic Therapy*, *The Writing Teacher*, and *Understanding Writing*. She received a B.S. in elementary education at West Chester State University and an M.Ed. in counseling at Boston University and has taken additional courses at the University of Southern Maine, Indiana University, and the University of New Hampshire.

William H. Teale is Professor in the Division of Education of the College of Social and Behavioral Sciences at the University of Texas at San Antonio. He has also taught in the School of Education at La Trobe University, Melbourne, Australia, and the University of Virginia. Professor Teale is the Chair of the Early Childhood and Literacy Development Committee of the International Reading Association, a member of the National Reading Conference's Student Outstanding Research Committee, and a recent President of the Alamo Reading Council. He is on the Editorial Board for *Reading Research Quarterly, Applied Psycholinguistics,* and *Reading Education in Texas* and on the Review Board for *Language Arts*. In addition, he has been the guest editor for two special issues of the *Australian Journal of Reading*. Professor Teale is the coeditor of *Emergent Literacy: Writing and Reading* and the author of numerous articles on teaching and reading. He received his B.A. in English at Pennsylvania State University and his M.Ed. and Ed.D. at the University of Virginia.